You
Saved Me,
Too

You Saved Me, Too

WHAT A HOLOCAUST SURVIVOR TAUGHT ME ABOUT LIVING, DYING, FIGHTING, LOVING, AND SWEARING IN YIDDISH

SUSAN KUSHNER RESNICK

Guilford, Connecticut

An imprint of Globe Pequot Press

Several names in this book have been changed to protect the innocent.
The rest of it is as true as it gets.

skirt!® is an attitude . . . spirited, independent, outspoken, serious, playful and irreverent, sometimes controversial, always passionate.

To buy books in quantity for corporate use
or incentives, call **(800) 962-0973**
or e-mail **premiums@GlobePequot.com**.

Text designer: Sheryl P. Kober
Project editor: Ellen Urban
Layout artist: Justin Marciano

Library of Congress Cataloging-in-Publication Data

Resnick, Susan Kushner.
 You saved me, too : what a Holocaust survivor taught me about living, dying, fighting, loving, and swearing in Yiddish / Susan Kushner Resnick.
  p. cm.
 Summary: "An extraordinary and literary 'love story' between a young mother and a much older Holocaust survivor that celebrates the unique and powerful bonds of friendship. It explores a complex relationship with someone from a different generation and socioeconomic background, and someone who happened to be one of the last surviving Holocaust witnesses of our time"—Publisher's summary.
 ISBN 978-0-7627-8038-9
 1. Holocaust survivors—United States—Anecdotes. 2. Jews, Polish—United States—Anecdotes. 3. Jews—Poland—Zychlin (Konin)—Anecdotes. 4. Holocaust, Jewish (1939-1945)—Poland—Influence. 5. Zychlin (Konin, Poland)—Anecdotes. I. Title. II. Title: What a Holocaust survivor taught me about living, dying, fighting, loving, and swearing in Yiddish.
 E184.36.S65R43 2012
 940.53'18092—dc23

2012014142

Printed in the United States of America

10 9 8 7 6 5 4 3 2 1

Who do you think this is dedicated to?

It's the leftover humans.
The survivors . . . I witness the ones who are left behind,
crumbling among the jigsaw puzzle of realization,
despair, and surprise. They have punctured hearts. They
have beaten lungs.

—MARKUS ZUSAK, *The Book Thief*

Late Fragment

And did you get what
you wanted from this life, even so?
I did.
And what did you want?
To call myself beloved, to feel myself
beloved on the earth.

—RAYMOND CARVER,
A New Path to the Waterfall

The Preface

JANUARY 9, 2011

You squinted your eyes so only a disk of color, slate-blue like an infant's, showed. Your focus at that moment may have been as limited as a newborn's, too, or you may have seen everything: her, me, the people you'd loved in that apartment by the sugar factory. Then, after you'd recognized that this was your last living moment, you dove. And we marveled: at the grace, the speed, the soundless break of the water—all in such contrast to every practice session that came before. For you had rehearsed this move, stepped right to the edge of the board, so many times, in your mind and in truth. You thought it would be loud, painful, clumsy. You were wrong. It was beautiful. Because of all that practice? Or because you finally, finally caught a break? Absolutely unknowable. Well done, my friend. Well done.

The Other Preface

I talk to strangers.

Everyone who hears the story of my odd and beautiful relationship with a quirky man who proved that the Final Solution wasn't final at all asks the same question: How did you meet him?

I talk to strangers, I tell them. And so did he.

Aron Lieb approached me in the lobby of a community center. When he started speaking in an accent thick with the Old Country, as if we were in the middle of a conversation, of course I spoke back. Our conversation lasted for more than fourteen years.

Aron was fiery and warm, irrational and perceptive, terrified and heroic. He was also my soul mate. My faux father, my son, my crush, and my cause. Before I became his health-care proxy and was declared his power of attorney, he would whisper into hospital-room telephones that I should pretend to be his niece when I visited so the nurses would reveal family-only details about his ailments. He frequently told me that I'd saved his life, but he saved mine, too, by giving me value as no one ever had before.

For much of our relationship, I focused on making sure he got the peaceful and painless life and death he deserved. I strongly believed that he should never feel discomfort again after what he'd endured both during and after the Holocaust, and I did what I could to ensure that. My quest led me to some David and Goliath–like fights with the established Jewish community. It forced me to suppress my temper and learn to be diplomatic with his caregivers, and it taught me to be patient with his fears and demands. Most surprisingly, my years as the manager of Aron's life showed me that being a good Jew has nothing to do with temple attendance or Hebrew fluency.

When someone dies, a long conversation ends. You'd been blabbing and blabbing to each other for years and then . . . *nothing*? How can you not be able to tell him how it ended, what that nurse said at exactly the right time, whether the evidence he promised to send proving heaven exists ever arrived? I don't know if I'll ever be able to stop speaking to Aron in my mind, but if I could have one more talk with him, this is what I would say.

Part 1:
Getting Here

January 9, 2011

These fucking people can't fucking drive.

They have no idea that my task on this Sunday morning is more urgent than all of theirs. The only mission of equal importance would involve escorting life in, but I know that's not happening because nobody ferrying a passenger with a baby crowning between her legs would be stopping at yellow lights. I'm certain I'm the only driver on Route 1 who's been dreading and preparing for this ride for almost fifteen years.

The sky is the color of a dull nickel. The snow has melted from enchantment to gloom. I must get to you before it's too late. I promised. I don't make a lot of promises, but I never break them. You should see the lurid secrets locked in my brain, corrupting it like leaky batteries, because I promised people I'd never reveal the stupid things they've done. Affairs, addictions, attempts to exterminate themselves. But my promise to you is neither ugly nor secret, though I'm not sure I've ever told it to anyone else. Just you, over and over.

I won't let you die alone.

You believe me, but you don't. What if they can't reach me?

"Do they have your number?" you ask.

"Yes. They have all of them. Don't worry."

I'm always telling you not to worry. Sorry about that.

"Write down your number again," you say.

And I do, in block print on unevenly torn pieces of scrap paper that you stuff into your pockets. I obey almost all of your commands, no matter how redundant and ridiculous. It's the least you deserve. How many other people have been rehearsing the lines of their deaths for most of their lives?

The light at this giant intersection turns green. The driver in front of me hesitates.

"Go!" I scream. "It's Sunday morning. Nobody's on the road!"

I am ready to fight, as I have been for the past four years of squiring you to the end. But the driver I'm yelling at can't hear me, of course, just like so many others who wouldn't hear me when I was figuratively pointing at you and screaming *Help him!*

You can't hear me right now, either, but I want you to know about this morning.

When the phone flashed your number, I knew what I was going to hear. Crullers. Belts. A terrible ache in your heart. Some request or complaint that I've heard five hundred times before. Funny how I almost always answer those calls in a tone of panic. *What? What?* I want to yelp into the caller's ear. But this time I sighed with annoyance because I was certain it was nothing but a reminder that you're still alive and that you want to see me. You know I come every Sunday, so why call? Don't you trust me?

The man's voice was alarmingly calm as he explained how it had played out.

"I'll be right there," I said when he finally paused. Who the hell speaks that slowly?

"Oh," the man said, snapping to life. "You're coming?"

I'm coming? Can you fucking believe that?

$\backsim$

So many times over our years together I imagined this day.

You did, too.

Imagined it and worried about it, over and over and over. For longer than I did, of course, but I bet I could have matched you in intensity.

On every trip I took, this specific worry cut the line before all the others. And it's a long line. I'm a bad traveler. I over-pack and try to control everything, which I know is antithetical to the purpose of travel. You're supposed to let go—especially on vacations—not my greatest skill.

The alpha worry was that I'd break my promise. It usually began with worrying about airport logistics. I'd calculate all I'd have to go through before reaching my destination. Cab to airport to boarding pass to luggage check to security line to wait to board to wait to fly to land to wait to baggage claim to cab to hotel. Then I'd reverse it. That's how long it would take me to get to you if the news came during a vacation or business trip.

What if this morning's call had arrived while I was reading the Sunday paper at a hotel restaurant in Red Lodge, Montana, instead of at my kitchen table in New England? You can't even fly direct from Montana, so I would have needed to add land-wait-connect in Denver or Chicago to the chain of impediments. That's a lot of hours. What if I didn't make it? What if I broke the promise because I was lying by a pool in Puerto Rico? I can't imagine forgiving myself for such self-indulgence.

Then I'd worry about money, as you always did, because booking an unplanned flight would be expensive. But I'd easily fold that one away as soon as I remembered that the Nazis would pay.

"I got this," I picture Hitler saying as he reaches for his wallet in his back pocket.

I'd worry if I were doing something important with my children, who always come first, despite your jealousy of that positioning. What if I was watching a play The Girl—as you still call my daughter, Carrie—had been rehearsing for months? Would I leave in the middle? What if Max was home with a stomach bug, but you were dying? You'd have nurses but he'd only have me, so how could I choose?

I'd worry the most during the summers when I was just over the border in Rhode Island. I never told you about those months I spent at rental beach houses instead of at home. You would have panicked yourself into misery. Not to mention the extra work it would have put on the staff, dealing with your ramped-up desperation. I still visited you during those summers, but stretched the visits to two-week intervals, and when you asked what I'd been up to, I'd say I'd been to the beach with the kids, which was true. I felt guilty about that lie of omission, by the way, but everyone agreed it was better for you not to know. Still, even when I was only a ninety-minute drive away, I worried about blowing it.

So wouldn't it be ironic if on this day, when I'm my usual half-hour from your side, I'm too late? Because of these fucking drivers.

AUGUST 1996

You picked *me* up—let's not forget that. I wasn't looking for love on
that bright and boring August day. I was just trying to hang on to my
mind, which at that point was like a wet bar of soap. I'd get it and lose
it and get it and lose it.

I'd been swimming laps just before we met. It was one of my less-
successful strategies for clearing up a nasty case of postpartum depression. Every other day I'd drop Carrie at preschool and then drive from
our bucolic town to the seedy city down the road, incongruous home
to a posh Jewish Community Center. While Max delighted women in
the babysitting room—an innate flirt, like you—I slapped the water,
as if I could beat the misery out of my muscles and leave it behind like
dirt from under my fingernails. I was balancing Max on one shoulder
while an empty car seat dangled from my arm when you noticed us.
My hair was still wet. You waited until I'd started to thread Max's arms
under his car-seat straps before approaching.

"Vhat's his name?" you asked.

I turned, summed you up as harmless, and answered.

"Max."

"Hey, Maxeleh," you said, your voice pitching higher. "What are
you doing, Maxeleh?"

You seemed to really like kids, which is why I asked if you had any
grandchildren. I figured you were seeking out strange babies because
yours lived far away and you missed them.

No grandchildren, you told me. No children, either. And your
wife had died four years earlier.

"She killed herself," you said.

Comedic beat. Wait for it.

"With chocolate."

Okay, not exactly, you explained. She had diabetes and wouldn't eat
right. Your eyes twinkled when you saw me grasp the chocolate joke.

"Where are you from?" I asked.

It was time for me to go, but I wanted to keep talking to you. I was
lonely and weak, but at that moment in time, you weren't.

"Poland."

"How long have you lived here?"

"Since 1949," you said, smiling down at Max. "After the war."

"You fought in the war?" I asked, stupidly.

"I was in the camps. All the camps."

All the camps. Maybe that wasn't completely true, but close enough. You'd lived in the Big House, the Yankee Stadium of camps, the White House of camps, the Taj Mahal of camps: Auschwitz. It was there that you became a number, as did everyone else who passed under the work-will-set-you-free banner and avoided the introductory gassing. I didn't realize until recently that Auschwitz inmates were the only ones tattooed. I'd thought they'd inked all of you. Now whenever I see someone with a Nazi-designed string of digits on their arm, I wonder if they knew you—if they crossed your path, shared your bunk, tried to steal your shoes.

Auschwitz was more of a stopover than a destination for you. Same with Dachau. You settled in longer at Birkenau, Auschwitz's sister property, but they were always moving you someplace. You resided in so many slave-labor camps that you can't remember all their names, and I will never be able to trace your moves with journalistic accuracy.

It will turn out to be easier to track your little sisters and the rest of your family because they traveled to death in a pack. But I knew none of this at our first meeting. Before you could dole out more hints, Vera arrived from the locker room. She'd been chlorinating herself in the pool, too. She had her stern Soviet face on, a face that said *Who the hell is this chick, and why is she talking to my man?* A biker's face.

You introduced me to your girlfriend, but when did we introduce ourselves to each other? I've rewound that morning countless times, but an exchange of names never plays. Maybe, as Max would later observe, it wasn't necessary. Maybe we already knew each other and you recognized us. Could you have been keeping an eye out for us before we were even born?

We walked out together and you two stopped to talk to another white-haired couple. I headed to my car, buckled Max in, and stalled in the driver's seat until you came close enough to hear me. I loved your contrast: so cheery for a Holocaust survivor. Nothing like the tragic heroes I'd read about or seen in movies. They never seemed to laugh, as if that ability had been starved out of them. You laughed more than I did. I wanted to know more.

I beckoned you over.

"Do you want to meet for coffee someday?" I asked.

"You buying?" you said, with the twinkly eyes again.

So I guess maybe *I* picked *you* up.

We decided on the following Friday. All week I worried that you'd stand me up. Why would this stranger want to hang with me? I knew I'd feel like an idiot if you didn't show, and inexplicably sad, too.

You weren't at the row of lobby chairs where the old men roosted while their wives exercised. I thought you'd blown me off; then I thought maybe I'd forgotten what you looked like and you were one of those dudes. But one was too fat and another had a mustache and none of them seemed to recognize me, so I kept walking. And there you were, a few yards down, all alone in your cap and glasses, waiting. You waved and jumped out of your seat.

You showed. That day and every week after. And while we blew on our hot coffee, you began to tell me everything.

JANUARY 9, 2011

I wonder if you said your line to the doctor this morning.

"Pain in my chest."

If someone had raked and bagged every word you ever said, these four would fill the most sacks.

There were variations, of course.

"The chest," you'd mutter, drawing your fingers across your sternum.

Or the full sentence, in a clear voice, as if you were making this announcement for the very first time: "I got a pain in the chest."

Dozens of medical professionals spent thousands of dollars investigating that pain. Their reaction is Pavlovian and, possibly, a law. The words *chest* and *pain* spoken in the same sentence in the presence of white coats cannot be ignored. They scanned and EKGed and enzyme-tested you over and over again, but they never found anything to fix.

I knew what was wrong.

Your mother. Your father. Your brother and his wife and their baby. Your sister and your other sister and your baby sister. The girl who brought you bread in the ghetto. Your grandmothers. The kids you sneaked glimpses of movies with. Everyone.

Lose one friend and the chest aches for months.

Lose them all and the pain never stops.

Why wasn't this obvious to the doctors?

I'd regularly float my theory by you when you insisted you needed to go to the hospital or have the nurses check your blood pressure twice an hour because you thought your heart was about to explode.

"Your pain is from your broken heart," I'd say. But you'd never respond.

Because you knew it was true. But if you accepted that fact—if you admitted that I was right—you'd also have to accept that the pain would never go away.

And now it might not.

SUMMER INTO FALL, 1996

By our second coffee date, you were talking about sex. Your stories involved leaving the displaced persons camp where you had lived for four years and working the black market. You got ahold of stockings and exchanged them for sex with German women.

"What about Jewish women?" I asked.

"No, no. You couldn't do that to them. They were good girls. I wouldn't take advantage."

It was revenge sex, the fragile tubes of silk giving the survivors power over the perpetrators. You and your fellow ex-prisoners essentially turned those young women into prostitutes. But of course, this being you, there was more love than vengeance. You fell for one of those German girls, a pretty blonde named Hermanie who lived on a farm and welcomed you into her warm bed. And at the same time, you pined for one of the Jewish girls back at the barracks. You wouldn't pursue her, though, because you had no trade for supporting her.

"I had nothing."

But even fifty years later, you still thought about her sometimes.

"She was cute, skinny," you said. "She was like you."

We were sitting in the Jewish Community Center cafe, which was more of a claimed space than a restaurant. Bordered by vending machines, floor-to-ceiling windows looking onto a grassy trap of a courtyard, and iron railings that separated the blond wood tables from the hallway, the cafe was where the mothers gathered after dropping their kids at day care or swimming lessons. I would often sit there staring out the window while preverbal Max sucked on a bottle, both of us wasting time before the excitement of retrieving Carrie from preschool. I was too saturated with anxiety to read, so I'd eavesdrop on the pairs of women leaning into each other with gossip, complaints, companionship. I've never minded eating alone, before or since, but I remember thinking it would have been nice not to feel so self-consciously friendless in that place. You cured that.

It must have been a Monday, because we met every Monday, Wednesday, and Friday, at 10:30 a.m. Even now, years since we broke that pattern, I still get hungry at 10:30, no matter what I've eaten for breakfast, or when.

Before we sat down, I told you I needed to pick up Max from the babysitting room. I invited you to join me. You leaned over the gate that kept the toddlers from escaping and waved at Max. He immediately smiled at the man with the hat, though he'd only seen you once in his life. You'd been imprinted.

Settled at the cafe, I drank scalding decaf and spread cream cheese from a foil packet onto a bagel that I shared with Max. You didn't eat anything.

"My stomach always bad," you said. "My mother, she send to me and the brother a package in the mail. Had in it salami. I was so sick with the typhus I couldn't eat a thing. He was sick, too, but he never passed up a meal. He ate it all."

This memory made you laugh. Most of the ones involving Bill did, probably because his story hasn't ended yet. When I asked the simplest questions about your sisters—such as what their names were—tears formed. But Bill got full sentences, as did his kids, "one a doctor and one a dentist." You, forever childless, were so proud of them. And of him, for seizing the American dream.

Max gnawed on his piece of the bagel while we talked, and you smiled and cooed at him. Until he coughed and you suddenly stopped and furrowed your brow.

"Don't let him eat that," you said, pointing to his mouthful of bagel. "He'll choke. Take it out!"

I told you he wouldn't choke, that babies always cough a little when they're stuffing their mouths—probably some congenital mechanism designed to slow them down so they'll live until the next meal. But you got so panicked that I had to swipe the glob of gummed dough out with my finger before we could continue discussing your years of starvation.

You stopped talking when Vera arrived. Though I'd originally pegged her as the uptight one, she turned out to be a surfer dude compared to you: relaxed and gracious. One afternoon that fall, the three of us gathered in our usual spot on an unusual day so you could meet the rest of my family. It was a Sunday, and you dressed as if you were going to church: a crisp, white button-down shirt and black leather shoes instead of your usual windbreaker and sneakers.

You shook David's hand. Very formal. Very masculine.

"Ah, you got a cutie here," you said. "If I was thirty years younger, you'd be in trouble."

You laughed, as if you were kidding.

"I know I would," David said. "She sees you more than she sees me."

Vera took out a small camera and sorted us into every possible group pose, including you and me, you and Max, you and Vera encircled by my kids and me. A few weeks later, when I visited her apartment, which was essentially yours, too, I saw that one framed and displayed on a bookshelf. She'd already concluded that we were frameworthy friends.

Wasn't it too early?

One morning at the cafe, I was the one who didn't want to eat. And out of nowhere—as if anything in our relationship was out of nowhere, but stay with me here—you asked, "Are you having a nervous breakdown?"

That freaked me out. I'd never cried in front of you or revealed anything about my temporary wrestling match with sanity. People who'd known me far longer than you had never realized I was struggling. But you knew, even without obvious clues. Maybe that's why you kept showing up. Have I ever thanked you for that? Those mornings when you gave me pieces of your pain and took pieces of mine were as powerful a cure as thrashing in the pool and sobbing with a shrink.

As my depression lifted, due in part to your consistency, I lost my splintery edges. I returned to smooth and solid, as if I'd been sanded. And with solidity came my old habits. I'm a journalist, so my default in any situation is to look for the story. I thought maybe I'd write an article about you. The idea of you and Vera, two aging immigrants who had found each other, appealed to me. You represented thick branches of the tree of tortured Jews. And like so many other people I've met over my many years of reporting—the single straight man with HIV who took me to his doctor's appointment, the woman I interviewed while sitting on the edge of her homeless-shelter bed, the extraordinarily wealthy lady who started to cry about her dead mother when I'd only come to interview her about interior decorating—I assumed I'd remember you well, but leave you behind anyway. It would have been impossible to imagine that I'd be the one in charge of your death.

JANUARY 9, 2011

I love you because you can't stop fighting.

You fight your horrific dreams and your worse memories. Your doctors and nurses. Your sister-in-law. Your pants and the belts that are always too big or too small. Men. The old people you claim are "gone with the wind." The headache you've had since before the war. Psychiatry, psychology, and drugs. Me.

I love you because you make me feel like a hero. But you're the hero. You're ninety-one years old, and before starting each day you must scoot the image of a man being hanged out of the way.

I love you because you hoard napkins. Because you still flirt. Because you hear everything that's said and not said in your presence, even though it seems like you're only listening to yourself complain. Because you know when I need you to come back to this world, and you come. Because you won. Because you picked me. Because you still fight.

Wait. Keep fighting. I'll be there in three traffic lights.

DECEMBER 15, 1919

You weren't supposed to live to see the beginning of the Holocaust, never mind its end. You weren't even supposed to survive your first month. Your mother, Zelda, delivered you at home, naturally, on a coarse feather bed with a midwife waiting by her knees. She and your father named you Shmiel Aron. Did she name you after a dead relative, as is the Jewish custom? Or did she choose the names because of what they signified? Shmiel, the Yiddish form of Samuel, means "His name is God." Aron means "exalted," but you didn't look nearly that promising.

"I was sick," you told me once. "I don't know what was wrong. Just sick. You know, how a baby isn't right?"

Your left eye was crossed. If you were as picky an eater then as you are now, you were probably refusing the breast, which would have left you scrawny and weak. Maybe you were fighting a virus or some congenital disease. But there was little your mother could do. It was 1919. There was no penicillin, no incubator. Babies die, the doctor must have thought; she'll have another. But Zelda loved her second-born as I love mine, so she did the only other thing available to mothers in her situation: She took you to the rabbi.

It should have been a happy time for Zelda. Her husband adored her, her firstborn was thriving, and her world was at peace. Poland had recently regained its independence and, for that blink of history, the Poles weren't bothering the Jews. But instead of reveling in the relative calm, she was trying to save a life. I see her wrapping you against the freezing cold and carrying you over cobblestone streets to the synagogue down the road from your house. Did your eyes tell all, even at that age? Did they bend at the corners with fear, an expression I know so well?

The rabbi looked you over and offered a solution. Your first name, Shmiel, would have to go. Maybe he objected because he didn't want a child named after God to die? Or maybe it had to do with the practice of assigning numbers to Hebrew letters; could the Hebrew spelling of Shmiel add up to something sinister? Who knows. But he subtracted Shmiel and added Matz, which means "gift of God" in Hebrew. So you became Aron Matz, exalted gift of God. And you got better. You would always be the runt of Zelda's boys, never as muscular or coordinated as your brothers. But you might be the toughest. That name change bought you almost a century of living.

OCTOBER 17, 2007

Dear Admissions Department,

I am submitting an application for an eighty-seven-year-old Holocaust survivor who has no wife, no children, and little money. I ask that you give his application special attention because of the difficult life he's led.

For the past four months, Aron Lieb has called 911 and gone to the hospital an average of twice a week for pain that no one can diagnose or treat. The general conclusion is that he is suffering from psychosomatic pain, probably a result of post-traumatic stress syndrome. He has refused long-term psychiatric care, though he is on psychotropic medications, which seem to do little for him. Though technically he is probably physically well enough to be alone, I, as his friend and health-care proxy, believe he can't live alone anymore due to his emotional issues. I also believe that he goes to the hospital so much because he is seeking the kind of reassurance, care, and social contact your facility could provide. When he is among people and medical practitioners, he is sharp and charming.

Enclosed are all the required forms except the financial guaranty. Aron has no one to take on such a role.

Again, I hope you will consider this a very special case. The world has treated this man horribly. I hope, at this stage in his life, the Jewish community can help to soothe him.

Sincerely,

Susan Kushner Resnick

I still believed in them when I wrote that. I believed they were good and powerful and used all their money to make things better.

That's a lie. I'd always been suspicious of the spending habits of certain large Jewish organizations. Why all that money for trees in Israel when there were hungry kids in America? Why all that money for fancy hospitals in that country when people in my country didn't have homes? Of course I believe that Israel is important as a symbol of our survival, but it seemed so much more important than America to so many American Jews, especially those with cash to throw around.

It was never a competition in your mind. The day after 9/11, I came to your apartment.

"Zoo baby," you said, pronouncing "Sue" the only way you knew how. "What did you do to the plane?"

You could joke because you weren't in shock like those of us who'd grown up believing our Americanness inoculated us against such unpleasantness. For you, it was just another really bad thing in a lifetime of really bad things. A horror, yes, but one that we'd live through like all the others. You were mainly offended that someone would attack the country that had been so kind to you.

"I knew the best soldiers in the world," you said. "They feel bad for you."

Americans saved you. America took you in and gave you another life, though certainly not the life promised in the brochures. Israel rejected you. You'd applied to emigrate, but after the doctors at the displaced persons camp found a spot on your lung, the Promised Land was unpromised to you. You would have given your money to your adopted country instead of Israel if you earned any extra.

At least I had faith that the Jews who kept all that money in the tribe would be there for a Jew in trouble.

Until they weren't.

Our first encounter with this nursing home was wonderful. That was a few years ago, after the loony bin, when I thought it might be a good idea to check the place out. A nice young social worker took us around. She showed us the atrium and the synagogue and introduced you to some hardy-looking men who spoke Yiddish with you. It looked like a resort, but it was clear to everyone that you didn't belong there yet because you could still take care of yourself.

"Y'all come back anytime," the social worker said. Not really, but that's what it felt like—warm and welcoming.

Time passed. I needed them because you were talking about guns. The Lady at the Party, dear friend of a dear friend, rich but so seemingly compassionate, convinced me I was right to expect them to roll out the red carpet for you.

What I got, after a whole lot of pleading, was Jerry Maguire. *Show us the money.*

I'd thought they were good and powerful, but it turned out they were only Great and Powerful, like Oz, who also turned out to be a disappointment.

JANUARY 9, 2011

Strange that we live in a *shtetl*, too. All these towns that I drive through on my way to your bed are home to just a tiny percentage of Jews, a reflection of much of America. But our town is an upscale, contemporary version of the little Jewish villages that were like freckles on the face of Europe before the Holocaust. More than 50 percent of our town's 18,000 souls are Jews. People used to say it was 70 percent, but that was before they built the mosque. On twenty-four square miles sit seven synagogues: two Reform, two Conservative, one modern Orthodox, and two ultra-Orthodox. I call members of the last category The Fanatics. I'm sorry; I'm just not fond of people who ban secular literature, don't recognize women's rights, and refuse to acknowledge people like me when we pass each other on the street because they don't think I'm a "real" Jew.

On weekends, our roads are crowded with people who could be ghosts from your lost world. Men with wildly long beards, black fedoras, and long cloaks tied at their waists like bathrobes float in clusters down streets on their way to pray. On Shabbat, their families join them: boys with hair coiled in *payot,* fringe from their prayer shawls dripping from under their white dress shirts; little girls in oversized hand-me-down dresses and teenaged ones forced to hide their sexuality with boxy denim jumpers and dark tights; and women under broad hats and shellacked wigs who push strollers no matter how hot, wet, or icy the ground.

We live in harmony with Christians and Muslims and Hindus, which would not have happened in Zychlin, but we also weather waves of anti-Semitism. Once a white supremacist group dropped hate literature on people's lawns. Swastikas have been painted on the outside of synagogues and the inside of high school bathrooms. Every year there seems to be some kind of Jew baiting from an opposing sports team: *Fucking Jew,* hissed through a field hockey player's mouth guard; *Come on, kike* barked from the lacrosse sidelines. Really nothing, compared to what you grew up with.

September 1996 (and Beyond)

I kind of wanted to sleep with you.

When a person is depressed, she doesn't feel anything. Then, as the medicine kicks in, she feels everything. The crush I developed on you was one of the first signs of life I'd had in a long time.

You must have felt something, too.

"Good thing I'm not thirty years younger," you'd say again. "David would be real jealous."

You would repeat a version of this threat often during the first half of our years together. Every time, we'd laugh at the line. But it wasn't really a joke, was it?

In my fantasies, set fifty years before we met, I am a strong American girl who holds you when you wake from your nightmares of being chased by dogs. I am the love of your life, the one who understands you as your real wife never would.

Or the affair would happen in the present, a *Harold and Maude* type thing, with our damaged, vulnerable souls melding. The forty-four-year age difference wouldn't matter because we could talk about anything, like when people of all ages fall in love and feel as if they've known the beloved forever. I would imagine running my hands up your weathered chest and it wouldn't even disgust me, though having those thoughts made me feel ashamed. You were an old man! I was a mother! What did sexual tension have to do with it?

You drove past my house several times a week just to see if my car was in the driveway, like a preteen pedaling his bike past his crush's house. And I made sure my makeup looked right before pressing your doorbell.

All this came before I saw that picture of you, which you accurately predicted would turn me on.

"You're gonna see me altogether different in the picture," you said. "You're gonna fall in love wit' the picture instead of me."

"I'm already in love with you," I flirted back.

It was taken when you were twenty-six, shortly after the war ended, probably by someone from the Red Cross. It looks like a passport photo, but the handsomest one I've ever seen. You had a strong jaw and sad, soulful eyes. Your combed-back hair was already receding, but it had a little wave to it. I didn't even know you'd been considered "dark blond" until I read it on your Dachau intake form, but then it was too late to ask you about it. Your mouth, wide and perfectly symmetrical in the photo, would someday smile again.

The attraction and fantasies sank as you aged, but they'd occasionally bob to the surface. Once when I was driving you to see a doctor, I felt as tingly as when a hunky high school boy had filled my passenger's seat years before. Another time, during one of our many talks about death, you said you were ready to die. I said I'd miss you.

"Maybe you'll come see me on the other side," you said. "We'll be born again."

"We could be married this time."

"We dream of things like these," you said with a smile.

THE ROARING TWENTIES

Back in your day, everyone hit the kids. Hell, back in my days as a kid, everyone did, too. But your household sounded like a super whackfest.

Your older brother, Mendel, would whack you and you'd pass that whack on to Bill. Your father whacked all three of you.

"It was a tradition—you know what I mean—when my father slapped me. Why did he slap me? Because his father hit him. Deserve, not deserve, he hit me."

You fought often with your sister Helen, who was the next youngest to you. I don't know if you ever hit her, but I doubt it, because hitting females wasn't part of the pattern.

"One time the father comes across to hit me. And the mother steps in front and says, 'Don't hit him, hit me instead.' And he never raise a hand to her, so I was okay."

Of course, that didn't mean your mother couldn't lay one on you. She went to hit you once but got blocked by your knobby elbow. She collided with bones instead of flesh, hurting her hand.

"Then I didn't come home for a whole two days. I was at my aunt's. I was afraid to come home to a beating from the father."

I asked what you did to make your mother so angry.

"Maybe I did something wrong," you said. "Who the hell knows?"

"Maybe?" I said. "I'm sure you did a lot wrong. You must have been a troublemaker."

"That's the way you talk to me?" you said, sounding a little hurt. "You're supposed to be my baby."

But despite all that whacking, you came from a good family. At least, that's what a lady who lives in Brooklyn, New York, told me. Her father was a poultry man who knew your father, a cattle man.

"They were nice people," she told me.

Then she needed to get off the phone.

"It's too much," she said. "My husband is sick. I can't talk of these sad memories anymore."

She was the last one to see Helen.

JANUARY 9, 2011

While the slow drivers continue to fuck with me at the final stop sign, I worry. You're not alone, are you? They've done a lot of disappointing things in that place, but they wouldn't leave you alone while you were dying . . . would they? Someone has to be sitting with you if you're in as bad a shape as the doctor implied. You were unconscious, he'd said. They weren't sure why.

Because if this is your last day and you are alone, I will be pissed.

All I've ever wanted from the people who run this place is royal treatment for you. You've had a bad life. You are entitled to a good death. Everyone who meets you should work toward that goal.

They haven't always, as we well know. But I'm trying. That's why I got into so much trouble before you moved here. And that's why I'm such a good girl now. I worry that if I'm too irritating, they'll take it out on you.

I feel completely responsible, though when we met, you were just my novelty. I guess I was yours, too. You used to rave to strangers about me.

"Isn't she a cutie? She's my sweetheart. I've adopted her!"

As we grew closer, our relationship became less defined. I didn't know what you were to me or why you were in my life, though I spent a lot of energy trying to figure it out. Then the people who should have known better than to screw with a Holocaust survivor had to obey the rules that prolonged your suffering. I stopped ruminating about the meaning of our relationship and started putting my mental resources toward getting you the finale you've earned. In my eyes, you are the king. And the king does not deserve to die alone.

1917

Theirs was your favorite love story.

"My mother had a face like a picture," you said, voice reverent. "Round. So beautiful. Not one spot on it. She must have been the nicest-looking woman in the whole city."

Your father certainly thought so.

His name was Leybish and he lived in Zychlin, Poland. Hers was Zelda. She lived in Plock, a big city with hospitals, factories, and about 30,000 residents that sat twenty-three miles from Zychlin, population 7,000. She was about twenty-two when they met.

"My mother, when she was young, she had an aunt lived in Zychlin. She come for, what you call it, a visit. And he saw her walking in the street. And he fell in love."

You giggled when you told me that story.

"He was so happy. She was two years older than the father, but he loved it. She had other fellas, too, what liked her. And anybody what wanted her, he beat them up."

Really? Come on—beat them up? I'm not sure I believe that, but I don't doubt the real obstacle he faced in marrying lovely Zelda: his mother's snobbery.

Your grandmother, named Leah, was educated. Though she was the daughter of a butcher, she had learned to read Hebrew, something most girls didn't do back then. She practiced it as she sat in the balcony of the synagogue surrounded by all the other women—women who could cook and sew and barter for a hen, but could not read a word of their holy books. Leah followed the prayers along with the men below her, her eyes trained on the black threads of Hebrew letters.

Or were they trained on the cattle broker in the third row?

Your grandfather learned to heal horses while serving in the Russian army in 1890 and spent his working life traveling the Polish countryside and tending to the livestock of wealthy farmers. The land-owners paid the young Jew well to keep their equine families free of disease and steady after injury. He was important to these important men who called him "doctor" even though he was not technically a vet. He began buying cows from farmers and selling them at cattle auctions to kosher butchers. He was one of few in Zychlin not impoverished. Maybe that's why Leah married him.

How does the song go?

For Mama, make him a scholar.
For Papa, make him rich as a king?

She and the doctor brought five girls and two boys into the world and raised them in comfort. They lived in a three-room flat in a building they owned. Leybish, the eldest, had followed his father into the profitable cattle business. But this beautiful girl he'd seen on the street was from a different class.

"What was the thing? See, my mother was from poor. My father was rich at that time. My grandmother says, 'I don't want you to marry her. She's too poor.' But my grandfather liked my mother. All the time my father wants to go see her. The grandmother looks like she's gonna faint. But he goes, takes the train to see her. And the old lady couldn't do nothing."

Leybish wooed Zelda to Zychlin with a promise and a bed. She lived with his family until the wedding.

"He almost didn't marry her," you said. "You see, I tell you. One day the grandfather, he gives my father five hundred rubles to go to the farms. He bought the cows, the calves, to sell at the market later. Before he gets to the farm, he sees a card game. He can make more money if he wins. So he stops and plays and loses all the money."

Your father stewed in town for a while, then went home and stood by Zelda's bed. She woke up and he explained the situation. He told her he couldn't marry her because she wasn't lucky: What else would explain his gambling misfortune? Zelda sat up in bed and yelled for her future father-in-law, who made his son track down the card players and get his money back.

They married in 1917. Leybish, who clearly lacked his father's business sense, continued to make financial goofs. By the time you arrived two years later, they were poor—Zelda as poor in adulthood as she was in childhood. But in your eyes at least, still beautiful.

ART: LOWBROW

My favorite movie and book share the same theme.

In *Same Time, Next Year*, a film based on a play, two married people, played by Alan Alda and Ellen Burstyn, meet at an inn when they're quite young and have an affair. Instead of breaking up or getting together permanently, they decide to meet in the same room on the same weekend every year. They remain constants in each other's lives and grow up together. She goes from a meek housewife to a strong feminist to a wise businesswoman. He goes from flakey to conservative to liberal to somewhat less flakey. Every time they meet, they laugh, fight, make love, and tell one good and one bad story about their spouses. Every time I watch it, I cry.

I used to tell people they must see this film, but now I don't because I worry they'll think I'm a fan of adultery, which I'm not. But that's not what the movie is really about. It's about knowing that there's one special person in the world who gets you, and still keeps showing up.

"You could always see through me," the man says.

"And I've always liked what I've seen," the woman replies.

We wouldn't be lying if we recited those lines to each other.

My favorite book also follows characters who have found their one special person in the world. I know as a writer I'm supposed to claim that my favorite childhood book was *Little Women* or *Treasure Island*, but no. It was *The Summer of My German Soldier*, a young adult novel by Bette Greene that tells the story of a physically abused Jewish preteen who finds strength through the platonic love of a German POW she hides in her tree house. He is the first person to acknowledge her worth.

"Even if you forget everything else I want you to always remember that you are a person of value, and you have a friend who loved you enough to give you his most valued possession," he says after handing her his great-grandfather's ring.

I love these lowbrow pieces of art because I've always craved such a connection. Doesn't everyone want to find the person who heals her loneliness?

My husband understands me more every day of our twenty-one-year marriage. My teenage children seem delighted when I crack my binding and read them new pages of myself. But we all, consciously or not, hide bits of ourselves from our loved ones. Such opacity is not possible with the ones who can see through us.

DECEMBER 2010

I tied the paper bib around your neck, embarrassed for us both. You were waiting for dinner. I was waiting for you to return from a trip inside your head. You've been disappearing a lot lately.

"This is like a lobster bib!" I said, trying to lure you back with silliness.

"Lobster, slobster," you said, taking the bait.

"Did you like lobster?"

"No," you said. "I never had it."

"If you never had it, how do you know you didn't like it?"

"She'd have it."

This is a clue. This is a bonus round on *Jeopardy*.

She'd? She'd? Alex Trebek is waiting for an answer. *Who is your late wife?*

"Your wife ate lobster?" I guess.

"She'd eat an old dog," you said.

Welcome back.

JANUARY 9, 2011

I'm so proud you made it to ninety-one last month. I was just shooting for ninety, but I guess you're more ambitious than you pretend to be. But even though you're super old and have made it clear that you're ready to die doesn't mean this is the end. You might be awake and bitching when I get there. This might just be a blip, like all the false alarms Vera has pulled: in and out of the hospital, but always stronger after the crises.

Still. You've been asking yourself for a long time what you're doing here. It's the eternal question in a survivor's line of work: Why did I survive? I once knew a rabbi who claimed that most survivors were bad souls who did something immoral—or at least nastily aggressive—that allowed them to prevail while millions around them died. I was already friends with you when he made that comment, and it pissed me off. It wasn't the only time I'd heard such a statement. Your own social worker once said to me, "He's very self-centered. That's how he survived." But they're wrong. You, despite your difficult personality, are not bad.

You've floated a couple of theories on what enabled your survival. The first is that you were used to starving. The more-comfortable Jews weren't equipped to go from roasted chickens and honey cakes to starvation. For you, slave rations were close to normal.

On Mondays and Thursdays, your mother shopped at the street market. The farmers' wives set up carts of eggs, butter, cheese, chickens, ducks, geese, potatoes, and onions. Merchants stood by big bowls of herring, figs, oranges, and lemons—almost all of it too expensive for Zelda. Though your father was a cattle broker, she could rarely afford standard cuts of beef. Instead, she'd buy meat from the cow's head or a live carp that she'd transform into gefilte fish or naked bones to simmer into soup. Shabbat dinner, always the most lavish meal of the week, consisted of a bowl of chicken soup with mashed potatoes on the side—just boiled and mashed, you told me, none of the butter or cream like I add—plus horseradish and challah. Sometimes your mother made the dough on Thursday, put it under a quilt to rise, braided it Friday morning, and carried it to the town bakery to bake. Other times, at least according to your memory, she bought the family's bread at the bakery or accepted a free loaf from the government. But it was never enough.

"Come a holiday, you need four bread on a table," you told me. "You only have two. What is a couple of slices of bread? Nothing. So a fella like me, I was hungry. Everyone was. Not only in my family. Over there, when you were poor, you were really poor. Here, now, poor is when you haven't got enough money. Food—everybody got what to eat. You never had a day with nothing to eat, have you?"

Hardly. I don't know what it's like to be poor. I grew up smack in the middle of the middle class, with a father who worked for an insurance company and a mother who took part-time social work jobs when I was old enough to heat my own dinner. We ate steak on Fridays, took vacations to Disney World, and kept the heat on high in our three-bedroom ranch house. If you had known me then, you would have thought I was a millionaire. Maybe you would have resented me as you did the privileged Jews in your community—the handful of people who owned most of the town's homes and businesses (they weren't allowed to buy land), but who wouldn't give you "the time of day," you told me once.

You ate bread with a little butter and tea for breakfast. Tea was big. A special dessert was a glass of tea and a piece of sugar. In the market, your father sometimes bought a big pretzel to eat with his tea. Was that his lunch?

"What lunch? What the hell is lunch?"

You can't remember what you did while the other kids in school ate in the middle of the day, but your brother Bill can't forget. He told me he hid so the other kids wouldn't see that he had nothing to eat. He was afraid to be teased. I doubt you cared as much what others thought.

But why go home for lunch? It wasn't the most pleasant place to hang out. You lived in a one-room flat equipped with a small stove that burned coal and wood for heat. Sometimes.

"When I was already maybe eight years old, I didn't want to go first to bed. You know why? It was cold. I go to bed and my brother comes and puts his cold feet on me. Then I thought I was gonna die! That's the kind of life it was."

You knew one girl whose family could afford electricity. You remember light coming from an oil lamp. A few businessmen had telephones and the doctor drove a car. The rest of you walked or rode in horse-drawn wagons. Fresh water came from a pump in the center of town. It took three minutes to get there from your house, but it must have felt much longer with a full bucket stretching your arms.

Your refrigerator was a hole in the floor. Your bed consisted of a wooden frame covered by a sheet, which was filled with fresh straw your parents bought from farmers and covered with another sheet. More sandwich than mattress. The family owned two feather pillows: eight heads, two pillows. There was one down quilt for the boys and one for the girls, which was fine because there were only two beds. You shared with your father and brothers. Your mother and sisters took the other one.

"When I think back, I don't know how they made the children."

Then there was the bathroom, which didn't actually exist. Few people in your town had indoor plumbing, though the wealthy did have keys to private outhouses. You shared yours with the residents of twelve apartments. It was a one-holed brick shack. Some people used the paper that oranges came wrapped in to wipe their bums, but your family couldn't afford oranges, so I don't know what you used.

You remembered that when you were little, you'd crouch over the hole so you didn't have to touch the edges. It must have been scary to go out there at night. Usually, you could use the pail in the house after dark, or hold it until morning before waking with the taste of smoke in your throat and racing to the outhouse. But nothing made the elimination situation worse than winter.

"God forbid you had a stomachache and it was very cold and snowy and you had to go outside," you said, laughing.

And to illustrate just how bad the bathroom situation was, how poor you were, and why you may have had a slightly easier time of it as a prisoner than people who'd once lived comfortably, you told me this: The bathrooms at the concentration camp were nicer than the ones at home.

ZUCCHINI SEASON, 1997

You liked to pretend that the Holocaust was no big deal. That you were over it. That it was just one of the many disappointments we all suffer.

"Say you have a boyfriend what uses you up a little, then lets you go," you said one day when we were alone. "Don't you feel sad?"

"Well, yeah," I admitted.

"You see. That's what I'm talking about."

Oh, right. Romantic disappointment is exactly the same as losing everything and being tortured while it happens.

But you couldn't always fool yourself. Not long after we met, we were on my deck, at my old house, on a Sunday morning. You and your girlfriend Vera had come for brunch. Carrie was running around with two giant zucchinis from our backyard garden. Max was crawling in and out of the slider doorway, his hair curled into soft wings that would be gone with his first haircut. You'd dressed up for us again.

"These pants cost a million dollars," you told us. "I couldn't believe it. How much should pants cost?"

"Probably less than a million," David said.

I acted housewifely, slicing the quiche I'd cooked and filling coffee cups. This must have pleased you. You used to lecture me on keeping a man.

"Listen good," you said during a coffee date. "A man likes to have a hot meal when he comes home!"

Not that you often did. You worked nights slicing meat. Your wife was asleep when you got home, so you'd cook something bland and dry for yourself.

After I'd cleared the table, we sat under a striped umbrella while the kids played in the sun. It was idyllic.

"I'm reading a book about the children of the Holocaust," I said. "Kids of people who were there. Like your nephews. It says they have a lot of problems."

"Nah," you said, waving your hand at me, a dismissive gesture I'd become familiar with. It meant *Shut up—you're wrong.*

"Their parents wanted them to be happy all the time," I continued. "They never let them be normal kids."

"No, I don't think so," you said.

"And they saw their parents sad all the time."

"What sad? I tell you something. When people come to a new country, they don't know the language, things are really hard. But pretty soon, they know the language and everything else is okay."

Ah—so coming to America in 1949 was hard. But nothing before that?

Vera winked at me after you spoke and shook her head.

"That's not what she means," she told you.

You continued to protest.

"When someone dies, you're sad. But then you go on and forget about it."

Nice powers of denial, sir.

Vera touched your arm. "You have nightmares every night of your life," she said.

Your face turned pink and you waved her off, too, as if you were angry that she had revealed your secret. Red bloomed on the rims of your eyelids and you reached a finger under your glasses to rub your eyes. You looked down at the million-dollar pants.

"Now I cry," you said, trying to laugh.

"Don't cry," Vera said, her voice more gentle now.

"I don't know why I start to cry then," you said, still wiping your eyes. "Why did that make me cry? I'm like my father. He'd look at something and start to cry."

"You're a sensitive guy," I said, and I patted your leg. But I wish I'd hugged you. Neither of us are big huggers, but I should have given you one that morning.

December 2009

"My parents.

And the girls.

They burned."

You were perched on the edge of your bed, still waking up from a nap, half in a different world. But you were talking to me, giving me this verse of horror. I reached out with a foolish question—"What girls?"— hoping you'd take my hand and pull me to that other side. I so wanted to see what was there, where you were, what it would feel like to stand in Zychlin or Auschwitz with you. But the question jerked you forward instead. You'd been looking at the floor, then you raised your eyes to me.

"Is it raining out?"

Studies, Schmudies

A Canadian study found that Holocaust survivors showed "marked disruptions of sleep and dreaming, intrusive memories, impairment of trust, avoidance of stressors, and heightened vulnerability to various types of age-associated retraumatization."

An Australian study found that decades after the Holocaust, survivors suffered from depression, anxiety, and physical complaints.

An American study found that "for some Holocaust survivors, impaired sleep and frequent nightmares are considerable problems even forty-five years after liberation."

And to sum it all up, an Israeli study found that male Holocaust survivors experienced more post-traumatic stress disorder (PTSD) than control subjects.

To which I say: Duh.

Of course you suffer from PTSD. How could you not? You didn't see a shrink in the displaced persons (DP) camps to flush out all those visions and losses when they were still fresh. You didn't see a shrink in America as those wounds scarred over and your anxiety, nightmares, and headaches got worse. You didn't even know you were suffering from a diagnosable problem back then, and neither did your doctors. PTSD wasn't a term until 1980, when, in response to Vietnam veterans' symptoms, the experts on psychiatry and suffering realized the phenomenon needed a name. Then they realized that it applied to people like you, too. They did all kinds of repetitive studies on Holocaust survivors: asking questions, swabbing saliva, drawing blood, tallying up the amount of anxiety-related chemicals your kind secreted. They looked at men, women, and children. They compared people who had been in concentration camps with people who had been in hiding. They looked at survivors with cancer and survivors with good jobs. But the bottom line of all the research was essentially the same: Holocaust survivors are prone to PTSD.

Again: Duh.

There are hundreds of studies confirming this obvious fact, but it seems like the people we run into—the people who should be up on this kind of data—aren't aware of it. Or they just choose not to address it.

Given what I know now, I'm not surprised by the ignorance and/or apathy. But when we started on our journey to Crazyland, I was continuously flabbergasted.

How many times did I say to someone in a white coat, "I think he has PTSD"?

How many times was my suggestion ignored?

JANUARY 9, 2011

As I got ready to drive to your bedside, I stuffed a different book in my bag. Maybe I'll read to you today; maybe it's finally time for the remedy of literature.

Why don't you ever read? You have all this quiet time and you never pick up a book. Your roommate reads. He wheels himself to the lobby and parks in front of something that looks like a microfilm machine, but is probably some kind of magnifier, and reads newspapers. That big lady in the wheelchair that took up the entire hallway used to read all day long. I never spoke to her, but I admired her because she put on makeup and read every day. That's how I want to go out.

For a while, I wasn't sure if you *could* read. When I showed you your town's *Yizkor* book, you studied the photos—and pointed to yourself in the group shot of survivors—but didn't even skim the words. Maybe you'd always been illiterate, or you'd just never picked up written English.

I'd sneak you tests once in a while, asking you to read from one of the many documents you filled out for the Germans.

"Looted assets: Two horses. Large wagon. Furniture and belongings."

Sure enough, you could read. You just chose not to.

One afternoon as we languished on the lobby chairs, someone began to throw dirty words around. Words like *bitch* and *slut*.

The voice was coming from around the corner. At first I thought I was overhearing a conversation, but then I realized the speaker was reading out loud. I excused myself so I could walk by and check out both the reader and the book. The former was a woman in her twenties—most likely a granddaughter. The latter was a biography of punk-rock feminists that called themselves Riot Grrrls. The granddaughter seemed to be in the middle of a chapter about raunchy performances. The grandmother seemed to be dozing.

I wonder if you heard the passages, or if you were too deep into your past to let anything in. The next week she was still at it, reciting more off-color chronicles of girl rebellion. They were racy in a way that both embarrassed and delighted me. You know how I love contrast.

Bitch and *slut* in a nursing home—what's better than that? Maybe I should try reading something tantalizing to you. I can see if the book I grabbed on the way out of the house has some dirty parts. If the word *vagina* doesn't wake you up, things aren't looking good.

But you've always hated when I try to introduce activities. Not long after you moved into the nursing home, I noticed the pile of games and playing cards stacked on some shelves across from the chair you've colonized. They were the type of things usually found in bed-and-breakfasts or beach rentals. They looked old, as if no one ever touched them, sort of like the building's residents. So one day, I figured instead of just sitting there talking about your blood pressure or dead people during our visit, we could pass the time with some recreation. You told me you'd played cards back in Zychlin. Remember—that kid cheated you out of your winnings, the one who later died of some kind of brain injury after his father beat him over the head?

"Hey!" I said. "Wanna play cards?"

"Cards?" you asked, with a face full of revulsion. "Are you drunk today?"

Fine. I guess that meant puzzles were out of the question, too. It also proved that we aren't a pleasant-pastime type of couple. That's too balanced for us. We're both extremists when it comes to conversation—give us something good or be quiet because you're boring us.

"Did you ever wish you weren't Jewish?" I asked.

You looked at me as if I was crazy—or still drunk—but then you jumped right into the pool with me.

"I did once," you said. "When I worked at the deli. I told a man and he started yelling at me."

I will not yell at you today. I will not ask if you want to play cards. I won't even read to myself.

FALL 2008
Teach us Yiddish words!

33

We were in the nursing home courtyard. Max was almost a teenager. He was getting bigger as you got smaller. We couldn't fill a visit with him sitting on your lap and eating borscht anymore, like we did when he was a toddler. At twelve, *you* have to entertain *them*. And I needed you to get fun quick. He was bouncing a ball, which meant he was bored already.

At first you seemed to think my request for Yiddish vocabulary lessons was *meshugge*.[1]

"Come on," I said. "How would you tell someone off?"

"*Ich hobn fant du.*" (I don't like you.)

That sounded kind of mild to me.

"What else?"

"*Gai in drerd arayn.*" (Go to hell.)

The bouncing stopped. The boy grinned.

Better.

"What other swears do you have?" I said.

Shmeggegge.[2]

"That's not a swear."

I wanted the real stuff. Shithead.[3] Asshole.[4] Something a boy could use.

But you're too much of a gentleman.

"*Ikh hob dikh lieb.*"

What's that mean?

"I love you."

Oh, dude—same.

COPYRIGHT 1974

This is not your first appearance in a book. The other one, published when I was eleven years old, is called *The Memorial Book of Zychlin,* or

---

1 Crazy.
2 Idiot.
3 *Kucker.*
4 *Shvantz.*

Sefer Zychlin in some language I should know. After years of research, I know this about the book:

- It's a collection of stories about and memories of your hometown, written by any and all survivors who cared to contribute. Such books were often compiled after the war and are referred to as *Yizkor* books. *Yizkor* means memory.
- It contains black-and-white pictures, some simple portraits of citizens, such as the one depicting an old man in a long coat smoking a very long pipe, but most are group shots: angry gray-haired men holding up a piece of paper and scowling, dapper young men (the same ones during better times?) gathered around a table and demonstrating the props of a meeting: ledger, document, cigarette; a mixed-gender group with little rectangles of paper stuck to their lapels and dress fronts; a sports team wearing striped jerseys, which, had they been allowed time to pack, could have saved the Nazis some cash; soldiers with rifles posing next to horse-drawn carts full of people and bundles; three skinny men standing in the snow wearing nothing except what looks to be wet pajama bottoms.
- It is blue.

I first saw the book in the library of the United States Holocaust Memorial Museum in Washington when I was hunting for clues about your history. This was back when you were still merely the subject of a potential story. It was quite easy for the librarian to find *Sefer Zychlin* for me. She even translated a couple of the captions as we stood between bookshelves.

"These are people who survived," she said, stopping at a group shot of twenty-five people.

I didn't even recognize the man in the top row, far right.

She told me one page listed the town's martyrs, which is what the authors called everyone who'd died during the Holocaust. I asked if she saw any Libfrajnds in the list. Yes, she said, there's a Mendel. Your older brother.

I couldn't take the book with me, but when I got home I searched the Internet to see if I could find one at a nearby library. Instead, I located a copy for sale on eBay. Two weeks later, it was mine.

The book is not only blue; it's also thin, but heavy, like you when I grasp your elbow to help you stand.

I thought I would find all kinds of stories and secrets about your life between those blue covers—stories about you and your parents, the cattle business and the creamery with the pretty girl, the temple and the fountain and the courtyard. Those anecdotes might be there, but not for my eyes.

I own the book of your life, but I can't read it.

It's written in Hebrew and in Yiddish, and I'm so ignorant that I can't even tell which is which. Not that I haven't tried. When I first got the book, I asked a friend's mother-in-law to translate it. This woman grew up in Germany, but escaped to Israel before it was too late. Presumably, she spoke both languages in question and would be able to Anglicize the whole book for me. She'd done translating before, my friend told me, and had lots of free time. She'd probably love the intellectual stimulation of a taking on a big project.

The woman agreed to look at the book and seemed enthusiastic about helping me. A couple of months after I gave it to her, she invited me to her house. I was so excited to finally learn about your childhood.

"I cannot do this," she said, handing it back to me. "It is too much. I cannot take the time."

She was apologetic, but wouldn't explain further. When I got home, I called my friend. She didn't understand her mother-in-law's sudden change of heart, either. Maybe, she guessed, reading the book was too emotional for her. Maybe her translation skills weren't as great as she'd assumed, and her mother-in-law was embarrassed to admit it. Maybe she really didn't have time.

Later, some other people, mostly Israelis I found through an online Jewish genealogy website, helped me translate snippets of the book.

None of them described your life. They're mainly about good times that happened long before the men with the rifles came to town. Few potential contributors survived the Holocaust, so the stories mostly came from people who'd left in the late nineteenth and early twentieth centuries, the decades when my relatives emigrated from their Old Country villages. At least that's what I think most of the book consists of. Like I said, I can't read it.

The pictures, however, are not all so irrelevant. After I bought the book, I showed it to you. I worried that it would trigger a nasty flashback—that you'd flip out after seeing those men in the snow. But you didn't.

"That's me," you said, tapping your thick finger onto the top corner of the group photo of the Zychliners who'd outlasted Hitler. There are seventeen men and eight women, all wearing business suits. Most of the men, except for you and a fellow with a thick neck and impressive pompadour, have covered their heads with hats. The faces have filled in and the hair has grown back. No one smiles or frowns.

CANDY

So, do you give the people in the nursing home candy bars because it's the kindest thing that was ever done for you, or because you see them as guards that you must bribe? I have always gone with the second theory. How else can I explain your franticness when the Snickers stash in your top drawer gets low?

"She makes my bed!" you'd say.

Or: "The Little Doctor—she's good to me."

At least the need to restock takes you out of your room once in a while.

You charmed the ladies who ran the gift shop, of course. When you still left your wing of the floor, your first stop was their minuscule place of business. They displayed the candy on one end and the coffee pod machine on the other. You'd collect $20 worth of Snickers and enough rolls of wild cherry Life Savers to get you through the week.

Then you'd pay an extra dollar for a coffee and ask the proprietor du jour to make it the way you like it. It isn't their job to make the coffee— that's why they set up a self-serve system. But the chicks can't resist a man who shuffles the hallways wearing a blazer and who refers to them as "my baby." Who knows how many *That's my baby*'s you collected, but one of them will stand respectfully when you go, in a mink no less, just as sad as the rest of us.

BACK WHEN POLAND WAS RUSSIA, THAT'S HOW LONG AGO

The *Yizkor* book that I can't read says there was a sugar-beet processing plant in Zychlin, and a pretty bridge where young couples would make out. I can picture the bridge, but I have to tell you I have no idea what a sugar beet is. I spent years writing a book about an American town that was also full of sugar beets, and even though I've looked up the term in several places, I still don't get it. Are they like regular beets except sweet? Are they like sugarcane, but called "beet" because of their shape? Are they sugar or beet, for God's sake?

Why didn't I ask you this question? Surely, you'd know the answer if this mystery crop really was part of your town's industry. I guess I cared more about atmosphere than the exports, so I pressed you to tell me whatever you remembered about Zychlin. It wasn't beets. It wasn't much of anything, really.

There was one big church and one synagogue, which stood around the corner from your uncle's house, but no hospital. If there was a fire, people ran around with buckets of water to put it out. Most of the streets were made of cobblestone or dirt, the houses, of wood, though some photos show homes of stucco or cement behind the people lining up for deportation.

Everything else I've learned about Zychlin comes from websites, reference books, or the *Yizkor* book, which is being translated for the public one frustrating section at a time. I buckle these facts together as if I'm writing a term paper so I can imagine where you spent your happy years.

The town is almost dead center in the middle of the country, about fifty-nine miles from Warsaw and eleven from Lodz, its closest big city. Around ten thousand people live there now, though there's no indication that any of them are Jews. I can't even tell if Zychliners like Jews these days. On a website that appears to be dedicated to children's welfare and is in need of "passionate" volunteers, there's a cartoon that looks blatantly anti-Semitic. It shows three bearded, hook-nosed, black-hatted men standing in a row. One is looking at a book, and one, who happens to be holding his *tallis* over his head (in case you weren't sure of their background), is screaming at the others. I write down the caption and type it into the Google translator. *People with passion,* it says. And now I'm confused. Are they saying that the Jews in the cartoon are respectably passionate . . . or crazy-passionate?

Other than this, there isn't much information about Zychlin that doesn't involve history. I learn that in your day, the water pump was right near the *mikveh,* the chicken slaughterhouse, and the tin-roofed, stone-walled synagogue. There were stores nearby, plus a church and a library.

It's hard to find accurate history on the Jews of your hometown. The creatively titled *Encyclopedia of Jewish Life Before and During the Holocaust* states that the first of you arrived in the mid-eighteenth century, and by 1897, you owned all of the town's 184 stores. One hundred and eighty-four? That seems high. It's not like there was a mall.

By your time, less than half of the town's 7,000 inhabitants were Jewish. The US Holocaust Memorial Museum says that in 1939, there were 3,500 of you.

Just as in our town, the Jews fell into extreme categories. We have the people in fur hats and wigs, and Reform congregations where non-Jews can touch the Torah. Zychlin in the 1930s had Hasids following an extreme leader who promised them miracles, and liberal Zionists dreaming of Israel. Zionism was big before the war. During the pogroms of 1918—Shoah Lite?—the kids involved in the Zionist youth movement organized self-defense units. Before the Nazis arrived, there was a Zionist pioneer training farm.

Beyond the city streets, your town was said to be lovely. You could smell jasmine and look at fields of corn. Same as here, minus the jasmine.

Zychlin's only brush with fame came in September of 1829, when Chopin attended a wedding reception in town. As of 1999, when they finally posted a plaque announcing his visit outside a palace across from the church, people were still talking about it.

There is no plaque, as far as I could determine, for Zychlin's most famous son, Abe Coleman. Known in America as Hebrew Hercules and Jewish Tarzan, this five-foot-three professional wrestler lived to be 101. He left town before the Nazis could get to him.

There is no plaque for you.

Once, when we were sitting in the chairs in the nursing home hallway, I asked if there was any place you wished you could go.

"I been to Poland, but I'd go there again, just to see what happened," you said.

I fantasized about taking you back. I'd book us a flight to Poland and hire a doctor to come with us because, obviously, you'd be too anxious to go with just me. We'd see how Zychlin had grown. Zychlin would see how you'd grown. It would be so cool.

But I never even persuaded you to take a ride with me to the bakery down the street once you'd checked into your last home. A trip to your first one was never to be—at least, in reality. Later, you'd go there all by yourself and tell me exactly what you saw.

SPRING 1998

The first time you spoke to me from a hospital bed it was no big deal. Like many older people, you'd been admitted for fluids and observation during a stomach bug. You called as soon as you were settled into a room to let me know.

"I had a baby yesterday!"

You were a remarkably healthy guy. Well into your eighties, you still had most of your original teeth, despite not having held a toothbrush until the Americans gave you one after the war. You'd had a couple of operations: the googly eye the Red Cross straightened, the gallbladder removal sometime in America. But you were hardy, so I didn't worry too much about your overnight hospitalization, though your call confused me. I still barely knew you. Why was I the first person you called? Where were your people?

You once had a wife, a brother, nephews, in-laws, a best friend, work colleagues—people from after, people who weren't burned. Where were they now?

Before the Nazis, your last name was much longer and had too many consonants. Your American wife convinced you to shorten it. Is it a coincidence that the new name, Lieb, starts with the word *lie?*

Bibi wooed you with premarital sexual acts and promises of financial security. Her father owned a grocery store that he vowed to pass on to you if you married her. She was overweight and destined to be a spinster. Her parents wanted her settled. You needed family, so it must have seemed like a decent bargain. You married her, wearing a sharp double-breasted suit. She wore green. I still have the picture.

Right after the wedding, the grocery went out of business. Weren't you angry? I'm sure you were, but by then you were best friends with anger.

JANUARY 9, 2011

I'm sorry to report that I'm wearing jeans again. I was in a hurry. I know how you feel about my clothes. You say, "You look nice," on the infrequent occasions when you approve. You like the knee-high black boots, even though I worried you'd have a Nazi flashback before I wore them in front of you for the first time. You hated the outfit I wore to Carrie's bat mitzvah. I was so happy to see you there, so touched that you'd deigned to enter a synagogue on my behalf. Of course, you took off before the reception and missed the klezmer band, but at least you paid your respects.

Let me remind you what I wore: a green Ralph Lauren cardigan that's still the most expensive item of clothing I've ever bought, and a plaid silk skirt made in Italy. The skirt flared and poufed, its light fabric changing shape as I moved. I got many compliments on that outfit, but not from you.

"What the hell are you wearing?" you asked that morning when you greeted me. "It's all wrinkled in the back."

You insulted that ensemble for weeks afterwards, until I finally told you to cut it out. I've since learned that you're much more into traditional tailored styles than avant-garde fashion. More Jackie O. than Madonna.

Your critiques of my hair when it gets too long are easier to take.

"Get the hair out of your eyes," you say, brushing my bangs aside. "A little trim in the back and you'll look good."

So it shouldn't have surprised me when one day you sneaked up behind me in the supermarket and tried to push your fashion agenda.

"Promise you won't give me a hard time," you said.

"I promise."

A few minutes earlier you'd popped out of a blood pressure booth as I wheeled my cart toward the bread aisle. You were pulling on your blazer and I was dressed in my usual worn, torn boy clothes. It took me until my late forties to realize that it's okay for a woman to dress nicely even when there's no occasion or no employer in sight.

We had hugged, kissed, parted. Now you were handing me a check.

"I signed my name, but you write in two hundred dollars and the rest. Go get yourself some spring clothes."

"I can't do that!"

"You said you wouldn't give me a hard time."

"Okay, okay, but I can't take that much."

"Vhat did I say?" firmly, like a father.

I took the check with no intention of cashing it. But I couldn't figure out exactly what to do with it. If I ripped it up, you would have been insulted. You're such a numbers whiz that you'd definitely notice the missing check at the end of the month. You should have been an accountant, perhaps in a fashion house. I did nothing with the check for a long time, but seeing it on the counter delighted me. When was the last time someone had bought me clothes? My mother in high school? A man never has. I spend my days buying clothes for other people, then washing, folding, and—in most cases back then—pulling those clothes over their owners' butts. For the first time in years, it felt as if someone was taking care of me. I had a sugar daddy.

Finally, you called and asked if I'd cashed the check. I pretended that I'd forgotten the amount you told me to write.

"You know what I said!" you bellowed.

"But I don't need it."

"Need, schmeed," you said. "Look. I get a check from the Germans every month. I appreciate what you do for me. You come when you don't have to."

The check from the Germans, which would get us into so much trouble later, was the one thing that gave you a little power in the world. You could never afford your own house, and I'm sure you never had one share of stock to your name, but you could buy gifts.

You finally agreed to let me write whatever amount I wanted on the check. I settled on $100, less than you'd offered, but enough to make you proud of your generosity. Then I went out and bought a white sundress with blue daisies on it, courtesy of the Nazis, who probably had no idea that one day they'd be paying for a Jewish man to buy a Jewish woman a new spring dress.

1928

The last baby in your family arrived. You were nearly nine years old. It was a girl—again—this one named Sarah. The house was full of kids. Mendel was ten and Berek, who would later live out the American dream as Bill, was three. Both of them would grow thicker and stronger than you, and more handsome. You said it, not me. You told me your father wasn't so good-looking and that you resembled him. I can see from photos that Bill was dashing, and you've told me that Mendel was, too. But I'll have to take your word for that. Who knows where photos of him ended up.

Helen was six and Hannah was two. With her black hair and eyes, Hannah would grow to be the most beautiful one, in your opinion. No one would ever marry her. Helen, you remember, was fat. You told me she looked twenty when she was only thirteen. Let's hope that bulk helped her later.

What did this new baby look like? You've never told me. She was one of the memories you only squint at, and then as infrequently as possible. I have pages and pages of notes on your life, and all I know about Sarah is that she liked to sing. You'd be trying to do your homework, and she'd be warbling a Yiddish song over and over. *My grandmother will bake challah. My grandfather will be healthy.*

I think that line is still stuck in your head.

Your mother sang, too, but she didn't read. She was completely illiterate. Your father could only read Yiddish. But like so many Jewish parents, they believed in education, at least to a point. Besides religious school, you all went to public school until fifth grade.

School wasn't bad. You were good at math. You had to speak Polish in class, but lapsed back into Yiddish at recess. On cold days, the teachers passed out warm glasses of milk and bulky rolls. Around the time the baby was born, you were walking your first crush, Braune, home from school. Her family owned a candy store. You carried her books.

You were a late bloomer with the girls, but you had your crushes. Even more serious than Braune was the creamery owner's granddaughter. She was one of several sisters.

"She used to talk a lot. She was a little shorter than me. Maybe she was five-five."

You were around eighteen years old when you started to notice her. You didn't shave yet, and you still had that crossed eye, but you thought you had a chance. You suspected her parents wanted to marry her off so they could move on to the next girl, get her off their payroll. Why shouldn't it be to you?

"You know, they used to say in Poland, when a man looks a little nicer than a monkey, he's okay then. As long as he's a man."

You were old enough to get married by then, but it didn't happen. Maybe you were playing the field, though that's doubtful, because you said you'd never touched more than a girl's shoulder before the war. Breasts were only for babies. It was American to use them for foreplay.

I've asked you the creamery girl's name several times. Once you told me it was Rose. Other times, you claimed not to remember. Was she the same girl who brought you bread in the ghetto? Wasn't that Rose, too?

They say the Nazis were really good at keeping lists, but I can't find a single Rose who would have been around your age and who lived in your town on any of them. Not on a list of the survivors or a list of the martyrs, as the memorial book calls them. No Rose from Zychlin in the displaced persons camps, or on a museum roster. But I also can't find the names of two of your sisters on any list, even though I know they existed. And that you've never gotten them out of your mind, either.

FOSTER CHILDREN

You're not my only cause. I also spend a few hours a month trying to help foster kids. Every six months, kids' cases come up for review, and a committee of two professionals and a volunteer from the community—that would be me—decide whether they're safe. We also determine if they're on the right track: adoption, reunion with parents, institutionalization, or foster home being the most common options.

I started this assignment when you were still independent because I wanted to see from the inside how difficult foster kids could be. David and I had seriously considered adopting one. My shrink says the idea appealed to me because I'd wanted saving as a child. Plus, I had a lot of suburban guilt to assuage.

We went to an information session for potential adoptive parents, but the group leader tried to scare us away.

"There is no way you want to get involved in this," she said.

Friends also thought we were nuts. One of them, a psychologist, said that at best, a foster child would screw up our biological children, and at worst, he'd kill us in our sleep.

Volunteering as a case reviewer gave me a more realistic picture. Many of the kids are terribly damaged, but not beyond hope, especially if they join new families when they're still in diapers. It's also good if they're significantly younger than the other kids in the adoptive family so they can get more undivided attention. We decided to wait until Max and Carrie were teenagers before starting the process.

Then you stepped in as the foster child understudy.

I still have a soft spot for foster kids, and sometimes consider becoming a state social worker, but as long as you're around, I'm full up on motherless dependents.

JANUARY 9, 2011

I'm here, on that steep hill that leads to the parking lot of the big cement building that is the final Promised Land for so many. It's too cold for anyone to be sitting outside, even the guy with the giant glasses who's always smoking out here in his wheelchair. Maybe later it will warm up and the robust residents will roll out. You used to like it out here, despite the fight you always picked whenever I'd suggest fresh air. But once I got you out, you relaxed. We'd sit here until the sun almost burned through our jackets, but we wouldn't take them off. Sometimes, between winters, it's nice to get too hot.

We sat on a cedar bench in the fall of 2008. The news I brought from the outside world involved Halloween, which naturally reminded you of Purim.

"I used to go trick-or-treat," you said.

"You did?" This I couldn't picture. "You dressed up?"

"It was the Jewish trick-or-treat. The one near Passover."

"Purim?"

"Yeah! Purim!"

Purim, like Halloween, is a vibrant celebration with a dark core. It's also a great day in Jewish history because it commemorates one of the few times the Jews actually kicked ass. The short version is this: Way back in the 400s BCE, in Persia, Esther was a beautiful Jewish queen, though no one knew she was Jewish except Mordecai, her uncle. Or was he her cousin? Reports vary. (Does our religion have a definitive answer for anything?)

Anyway, Mordecai didn't hide his Jewishness. He flaunted it by refusing to bow down to Haman, the king's Jew-hating prime minister (or nobleman—again, it depends on who's telling the story). This really pissed off Haman. He tattled to the king.

"Can I kill all the Jews?" Haman asked.

"Sure," the king said.

But before they could get the cattle cars running, Mordecai convinced Esther to come out as a Jew and talk to the king.

"Will you *not* kill all the Jews?" she asked.

"Sure," the king said.

Okay, it was a little more complicated than that. The king was in a Jew-liking mood because he'd just found out that Mordecai had allegedly saved his life earlier by snitching on some would-be assassins. Haman was in the doghouse for wanting to hang Mordecai after the refusal-to-bow incident. In the end, Haman hanged and the Jews received permission to defend themselves against the anti-Semites Haman had riled up, which resulted in a lot of dead Persians.

Jewish children in your day still celebrated this victory over evil. And those memories made you laugh harder than I have ever seen you laugh.

Back in Zychlin, you and your posse went door to door, singing Yiddish songs for cash on Purim. Since observant Jewish adults are encouraged to drink heartily to celebrate Purim, I assume you kids were unsupervised.

"We went to the rabbi's house first. He'd give me a nickel. You could make two dollars on a good Purim."

This memory grabbed the hand of another and pulled it to the surface. Suddenly, you were grinning, and just as suddenly, giggling.

"One day Mendel and I were in back of a house and he knocks on the door and . . ."

Your words got buried under your laughter. You couldn't get the story out because you were back there in somebody's yard, cracking up with your best friend. It took three tries for you to tell me that Mendel had banged his fist on this door and then both of you and some other kids ran away—a classic ding-and-ditch—before the owner opened the door and started to yell. I guess you came back to the door because the man asked who had knocked, and Mendel pointed to one of the other kids, so he got in trouble instead, and it was so funny, so, so funny, that eighty years later your eyes were twinkling and your mouth was turned all the way up like a face in a child's drawing, and you practically peed your pants from convulsing so hard.

Did that happen on Purim, too? It doesn't matter. Purim released the memory, let you step back into the light of your childhood.

You weren't around for your town's last Purim, though you may have spent that day longing to be home, laughing again with Mendel. You wouldn't have known how lucky you were to be excluded from the town-wide activities. Because on Purim of 1942, Haman returned.

DECEMBER 26, 1993

My favorite love story is yours. You'd just turned seventy-four, but it was the first time you were ever set up on a date. Your late wife's cousin, Lakey, arranged it after you told her you wanted to meet one of the many Russian women in her building. Your wife had been dead for a year, and you wanted company. But why a Russian woman? You'd always regretted not marrying that Old Country girl you'd met in the displaced persons camp. Was this your way of rectifying that mistake?

Lakey thought of a few candidates. She visited two to make your case. Their friend Vera happened to be visiting, too. The other ladies weren't interested in you.

"I'll meet him," Vera said.

She was seventy-one and had recently arrived in America after years of Soviet oppression. She wanted to meet Americans and learn to speak English well. As a former professor of German, she knew the only way to master a foreign language was to speak it. At the very least, she'd get some practice on your date.

You dressed carefully. I can imagine the outfit: button-down shirt, wool sweater vest, neatly pressed trousers, and shined shoes. Maybe even a tie. The green hat from your brother-in-law, The Millionaire.

You would have driven the Buick Skylark from your old people's apartment building to hers. Yours was a little nicer, with its indoor gardens and chandeliered dining room. Hers smells of mothballs and stuffed cabbage. It was a long walk down several hallways to her apartment. Finally, you stood outside the door. Number 141.

You loved that. Your first blind date, and the woman's apartment number is the same as the one on your skin. For fifty years, every time you'd taken off your shirt at night or reached out to adjust your side-view mirror on a summer day, you saw those numbers, plus three more: 141324, the brand the Nazis gave you when they thought you were theirs.

Was it a sign? I like to think so.

"The first times I look at him and thought he won't come to me next time," Vera said. "He is younger than me, and so handsome."

But she was wrong about two of those things. After talking for about an hour, you asked her to go to dinner with you the following week. By the third date, you rarely went a day without seeing her. The first kiss came about a month after you knocked on her door. Shortly after that, you stopped sleeping at your apartment.

You settled into a sweet routine. To McDonald's for coffee almost every day. To the pancake house every two weeks. Dinners at a famous old-school steakhouse where you ordered fish and she ordered chicken. You shopped at all the local discount stores, where you liked to buy her things: a necklace for no reason at all, a VCR, a bigger mattress. She, in return, gave you a new family. Her children and their children welcomed you into their lives.

The relationship wasn't perfect, of course. You got cranky and yelled at her sometimes, which her esteemed husband had never done, but you always apologized and she always forgave you. It wasn't like the vicious fights you'd had with your wife.

"With Vera, I appreciate, she appreciates," you told me.

"He takes care of me," she said.

And she takes care of you. Even the person who's known you the longest noticed that.

"She knows how to handle him," Bill said. "He's happy. He's happier than he was with his wife—one hundred percent happier."

You and Vera once argued when I was over for a visit. As you both forced those strange hard candies on me, you bickered about when you'd give up your apartment and move permanently to her building. It was a classic girl/boy fight, and you hung on for a while, then gave in suddenly and unexpectedly as you always do. Vera thanked you. You tried to hide your aw-shucks smile.

The most romantic thing about you two is that you connected despite being so different. She is the highly educated daughter of doctors. You are the fifth-grade graduate raised by a woman who couldn't read. She translates poetry while you watch wrestling. She has greatgrandchildren and you have nobody. You have nothing in common except the fact that you both survived the great twentieth-century attempts to snuff out the Jews. I liked that when we first met; you were both living embodiments of Jewish history, symbols of our endurance. I guess you still are, though so much has changed. She is in this building, too, but you don't see each other much. She's lost all that English you helped her learn.

ALL THE DAYS, OBVIOUSLY

Then there was God, theory number two on why you survived.

You've speculated that you survived because the Lord above was on your side that day of the potato shipment—and during the entire last year of the war.

You and I both believe in God more than we believe in Judaism. I think that makes us uber minorities.

I run into lots of tribespeople who jump the ritual hurdles of Judaism but think God is a silly concept. There's even a branch of Judaism called Reconstructionism, whose members embrace Jewish traditions but reject the idea of God as a "being." I'm the opposite. I think the stories, rules, and rituals are mostly ridiculous, but I have never stopped believing in God, even as my image of her has evolved.

My God used to look like the full-body figure from my parents' copy of *Gray's Anatomy*. Both of them were biology majors in college, and their *Gray's* textbook was one of the coolest items in our house. I would leaf through it regularly, always ending up at the colored cellophane overlays. Placed over the outline of a man, they added bones, muscles, or veins to his shape. The figure had no face or hair, just a form and innards. That's how I imagined God, except he (God was still a man back then) sat on the moon, posed like Rodin's *The Thinker* sculpture. If I opened my bedroom shade at night and looked over the tops of the oak trees, I could tell him all my problems and ask for help.

I always thought God was good, and kind, and not scary, so I don't get the way the crowd ass-kisses God during Jewish services. Why all the praise and thanks, every other page? *You're great, you're great, you're great*, the words declare; *of course you're our one and only*. The God I believe in isn't that insecure.

Or powerful. I don't believe that God answers our prayers anymore, though I throw one out there every now and then as a test. Now I believe she's impotent to control the world; that she made the humans and gave us free will. This helps me explain why she didn't stop the Holocaust. According to my version, God doesn't start or stop anything, but I think she stays with us during those times when we need to pray. She holds our hands and props us up, helping us to keep going. Or she spectates on the good times.

Like when I was watching Carrie run through a dress rehearsal of her bat mitzvah service and felt myself fill up with warm, gooey pride. Carrie was knocking it out of the park. She and the rabbi went through the prayers on the *bimah,* and I sat in the third row and God hovered on the ceiling. Crazy, right? But without the people and the judgment I perceived coming from them, I felt God's presence. I thought it was a turning point—that from then on I'd sense her whenever I entered that room and that I'd love the Jewish experience. But I never found her there again. Maybe she doesn't like crowds.

God looks different to me now, too. She's developed from an outline with blood vessels to a woman with lots of curls who wears a white toga and has the face of my friend, Abby, who helped people with AIDS in a godlike way before she died much too young. But even with the gender reassignment and abbreviated powers, God is still the same entity who lived outside my window. The same God who might have seen how content I was at age fourteen to wind a string of silver garland around a Christmas tree with my friend's warm, happy family. The same God who kept me company as I sat outside in the cold sunshine while my playmates confessed their sins in a Catholic church that looked like a giant birthday cake. The same God who you think pushed us together.

One day, I was trying to convince you to let me be your health-care proxy and you were trying to come up with reasons to refuse. You'd already told me that all you needed was for David and me to visit you if you got sick.

"What if you have a stroke?" I asked.

"So what? I won't know what's going on."

"What if you're in a coma? They'll keep you hooked up to machines unless someone tells them not to. Is that what you want?"

I knew you didn't; you frequently didn't even want to live while you could walk and talk. I knew I had you there. You said nothing.

And then: "God sent you to me. That's enough."

Enough for what?

"The day I met you and little Maxeleh, God was with me. Just like when I go to Birkenau."

Impressive debate tactic. How was I supposed to compete with that?

I was stunned by your words. *God sent you to me.* Who says something so beautiful in the midst of complaints and irrationality?

God put her hands to her chest. Even she was moved.

1929

Despite losing most of his money, your Zychlin grandfather kept his property and enough cash to give each grandchild five cents when he or she was born.

He gave you so much more.

When you were with him, you weren't just one of six; you were the only one. So you spent as much time as you could with him. In the winter, you sat with him as he smoked his pipe and listened as Yiddish love songs played from his gramophone. In the summer, the two of you would walk to the town creamery. He would bring his own plate and order a scoop of cottage cheese and a scoop of sour cream, then take them back to his apartment where he'd stir them together and complete the concoction with a sprinkle of scallions. That taste—tart, creamy, oniony—would bring you back to your grandfather's side for the rest of your life.

You'd have sleepovers with him just as I did with my grandmother. Those were the best, weren't they? I got to sleep in my grandmother's bed, with her on one side and the beautiful bottles of perfume that spanned her dresser on the other. Everything was fragrant and orderly in her apartment, which probably explains my attraction to department-store perfume counters. No, I don't want a sample, I tell the ladies. I just want to feel safe again for a few minutes.

Your slumber parties were just as comforting to you. Sometimes you climbed into bed with your *zayde*, snuggling against him and rubbing his back until you both fell asleep. Then his snoring would wake you up. Knowing you'd never get back to sleep—you've always been a light sleeper—you'd run through the dark neighborhoods to your own crowded bed.

The bond broke when you were ten. A doctor found cancer inside that good man, and made him comfortable until he died. He was only fifty-nine years old. It was your first experience with death. You lost the one person who made you feel special. That must have felt like the end of your world. Little did you know that your intro to death would turn out to be your only normal loss. Your best death. The first and last innocent one.

JANUARY 9, 2011

I park the car and run—through the sliding doors, past the front desk, left at the fish tank, right after the gift shop, straight past the art gallery, the elevators, and your empty chair. Down the long hall, last door on the left, bed across from the bathroom, you.

Alone.

Are they fucking kidding me? You're unconscious, plugged into oxygen, and *alone*?

The room looks different—not as yellow as usual. Did they paint? Oh, I see why: The bright light over your bed is on, as if you're a hospital patient. And there's a big canister of oxygen on the floor. Everything else is the same as when you went to sleep. An unfurled roll of wild cherry Life Savers sits on your night table next to a plastic cup of water. A shadow of cherry pink from your last sip rings the straw.

Your world has shrunk to half of a room. Remember when we first came and you didn't seem to belong at all? Everyone else seemed more diminished and addled. You needed to be here, of course—the guns, the pills—but after you moved in, you'd talk about leaving all the time. You wanted to tour your old life: go out for steaks, take a ride to the IHOP, come to my house to look at your summer shoes. You wanted David and your lady friend to join us. But whenever I tried to plan such an outing, you always said you felt too sick. Maybe you knew it would be too hard to come back if you let yourself leave. And the way you look right now, I'm pretty sure steaks are out of the question.

They couldn't assign someone to sit with you until I came? That was part of the promise—that you wouldn't die alone. Though I never specified what time frame dying encompassed, this seems like a critical interlude. But maybe it's not. Maybe you're not really dying. Maybe they can tell that this is just an episode of some kind, no matter how nervous the doctor seemed. What do doctors know? Nurses are the ones who run the show.

You're sleeping with a plastic mask over your nose and mouth. It's attached to you with a green elastic strap that digs into your cheeks. You're wearing an undershirt and you're partially covered by a sheet and a blanket. I pull them up to warm your shoulders.

"I'm here now," I say, dumping my stuff and pulling the chair close.

It looks like you can't catch your breath—like you ran too fast for too long.

I reach under the sheet to take your hand. Your smooth white hip is bare, all of you from the waist down, naked. Why did they keep the shirt on you?

Your hand is warm and clammy. Your breaths are fast and sharp and shallow. They seem to take a lot of work.

MAY 1976

I should have become a bat mitzvah during this month of this year. I was thirteen, and a member of the first generation of Jewish girls who were expected, rather than allowed, to step up to the ark. Boys, of course, have marked their thirteenth year with a bar mitzvah celebration of some type since around the sixteenth century. Even you had one, though it wasn't the fancy ordeal it's become in America. You simply reported to the synagogue on a specific Saturday morning in 1932 and repeated some Torah passages after the rabbi read them. Or so your memory tells you. I suspect that you knew your portion by heart.

This ritual bestows upon hormonally freaked-out teenagers the Jewish equivalent of adult responsibilities. After proving they're capable of reading from the Torah, they are expected to obey all the commandments and to behave morally like a Jewish grown-up, whatever that means.

I did not become a bat mitzvah, or as we called them back then, bas mitzvahs. It was before the pronunciation authorities changed the way we speak Hebrew. The "s" ending, as in *bas* or *Shabbas,* was too reminiscent of the way European Jews said the words. European Jews, the thinking went, had let themselves get killed. Therefore, the European Jews' way of pronouncing Hebrew words was wimpy. The "t" ending—*bat, Shabbat*—was Israeli. Israelis were tough. Israelis ended their words with hard consonants. Israelis would have killed back.

But however you want to pronounce it and however you want to say it—the casual and customary "had a bat mitzvah" versus the grammatically correct "became a bat mitzvah"—I didn't. I am deep into my forties, but in the eyes of the Jewish community, I am still a girl.

Girls of the seventies had equal-with-the-boys ceremonies to mark their coming of age as Jewish adults. No longer scheduled on Friday nights or done without a Torah, this was the real thing. I guess I should have been proud to finally have such an opportunity, but I couldn't handle it. I have always been terrible at foreign languages. I took five years of public school Spanish, plus two years in college before I could finally speak a few fluent sentences. And even then I had to be drunk to get the verbs right.

I started Hebrew school in fourth grade as most Reform Jewish kids do, but I seemed to be the only one who didn't catch on. I was okay when we read aloud as a group; all it takes is some mumbling spiked with a few *ch, ch* mucus clears of the throat. But reading aloud by myself was a disaster. I always got it wrong, so the other kids knew I was the dope of the class. This, of course, was humiliating and gave me good reason to fight going to class. *Please, please, please, please, please don't make me go,* I'd whine. They still made me go. Eventually, the teacher figured out that I knew nothing and suggested a tutor. This opened a series of negotiations between my parents and me. I agreed to work with the tutor if they *please, please, please* wouldn't make me go back to Hebrew school. They demanded that I finish the first grade of Hebrew with the tutor, but they wouldn't force me to continue. If I didn't continue, I couldn't have a bat mitzvah.

Wow, ten-year-old me thought. God *is* good.

I mean, I didn't need the money. My parents paid for my food, shelter, clothing, and David Cassidy records, so why slog through what was clearly just a money-making enterprise? I don't remember hearing an explanation about the important reasons to go through the ritual, but I was a visual learner and had watched my older brother become rich enough to buy his own TV after his multi-partied event. He seemed happy with the exchange—years of suffering for a TV— but no amount of money could inspire me to endure three more years of Hebrew school. I spent the second half of fourth grade meeting weekly at a card table in my family room with the tutor, a young guy with lanky arms and a lanky mustache who was also, improbably, the principal of our religious school. I hated those hours, but at least only one person was witnessing me as the biggest dope in the room. When the year ended, I was poor, but free.

My parents never made me feel bad about it. They were probably so exhausted from the Hebrew school battles that they felt more relief than disappointment. I was a lot of work for them. Ours was a household saturated with the unhappiness of two people who shouldn't have married each other. I was the charcoal absorbing all that emotional venom. As a result, I became whiney, anxious, needy, and insecure. Hebrew school proved a great outlet for these charming traits.

But part of me wishes they'd forced me to get up on the altar in a lovely dress and recite a few paragraphs of Hebrew. It might have given me some much-needed confidence, and shortened the long list of reasons that I feel like a failed Jew.

October 2000

I expected disapproval when I told you we'd gotten a puppy. I thought you'd think it was stupid, indulgent, one of those nuisances that Americans trouble themselves with.

Instead, I got reverie.

It turned out that you, like boys from all lands and eras, had had dogs to adore. Dogs you could hug your bad day into. Dogs whose fur hid tears. Dogs who cracked you up.

There was Lika, a soft, white mutt who wandered the streets at will. She swelled up one season, curled into a ball, and delivered puppies. Your parents let you keep one of them. You named him Aps.

"One day, we leave him in the house and go away. He jumps through the window and comes to us, miles away. Just shows up and starts barking."

Humph. There were dogs. That's so normal, so undramatic. I never think of the people in the sepia photos letting their dogs in and out of the house.

That was one of the good parts of your childhood. There were others, too. Okay, so you stood on the sidelines while the more-coordinated kids played soccer because you were, in your words, a *schlemiel*—a klutz. And you couldn't play in the snow because you didn't have warm-enough clothing. But when spring finally came, you rented bikes. Fifteen cents for fifteen minutes of real happiness, even if you did fall forward and grate your palms once in a while. On Sundays, you and your friends tramped to the woods for picnics sponsored by the Jewish youth organization. And every month, the local Yiddish theater company put on a show in your school building. You couldn't afford a ticket, but nothing stopped you from creating your own balcony seat on a windowsill with a decent view of the stage. No such complimentary seating existed at the cinema, but a cousin had enough money for a ticket to the weekly Polish movie. You'd watch it through his eyes as he re-created the entire film for all the poor kids.

And your summers—your summers were paradise! It was the poor Polish equivalent of rich American summer camp. For ten weeks your whole family left the city and camped out near an orchard about fifteen miles away. You slept in tents, pooped in ditches, pranced around barefoot, and learned what it felt like to be full. You devoured eggs for breakfast, chicken for dinner, and bowls of milk and potatoes during lunch breaks. That's right: lunch.

Between meals, you could eat as you worked. You and your siblings climbed trees to pluck fruit. When the bushels got fuller than the trees, your father would pack the harvest into sacks and drive it to Lodz, where merchants bought it, loaded it onto freight trains, and sold it to city folks for good money. Your father earned a percentage of the farmers' profits. You sometimes went with him and earned a city bagel.

Farm life didn't make your family rich. You still wore cheap, store-bought clothes that ripped before they got too small (tailor-stitched frocks were only for privileged people). Your parents still argued about money. But at least you got to be a normal, dog-owning kid for a little while.

June 2009

I started writing imaginary letters to your mother a few years ago. She was the first one in charge of you and I am the last. She brought you into the world and I'm guiding you out. We are both mothers. If our fates had been reversed, I'd want to know what happened to my son.

Dear Mrs. Libfrajnd,

I watched Aron sleep this afternoon. It was early summer outside, but late fall in his room. He'd closed the curtain that divides his side from his roommate's side so he didn't have to see him, but that blocked out all daylight, too. He took deep, quick breaths, like babies do, which made his belly rise and fall heavily beneath his undershirt. He didn't make any noise, but his eyes were clenched and he was frowning.

He doesn't frown when he's awake. He glares sometimes, or grimaces. He hides his lips altogether when he gets weepy, and he has a big, wide grin when he's happy. His eyes gleam. But he's not a frowner. That must come from what he sees in his sleep.

He's eighty-nine now and I'm doing all I can to get him to ninety. He doubts he'll make it. He complains a lot about the pain in his chest and stomach and now in his hip. Last week, for about the two-hundredth time since I've known him, he told me he thought he was dying. It terrifies him, but he knows it could be worse.

"At least I'm not in the gas chambers, like everyone in my family," he said.

All except one. I call that one every so often with updates about Aron, which I'm not entirely sure are appreciated, but which I feel obligated to share. That other child of yours is doing okay: married with kids who had kids. The family has money—a typical American success story.

Not Aron, though. His life's been harder than most since the last time you saw him. I bet he would have fared better if you'd been around to nudge him away from some people and situations and toward others, like you did when you banned him from seeing Mendel after the iron-stealing incident. He needed management. I suppose he still does. I'm doing the best I can.

Sincerely,
Susan Kushner Resnick

1926, GIVE OR TAKE

I wish I'd met your best friend Mendel. I want to watch the film of you playing together every day of your childhood, wandering the streets, going to parties, riding bikes. You clicked as soon as you met as little skullcapped boys in religious school. He was tall, a few months younger than you, and lived a block away. Improbably, his family was even poorer than yours. With eight kids to feed, they couldn't afford a luxury like public school.

"You had to buy the books, pencils, pens, and this was very expensive," you said. "And you buy a Polish book to read, was two zlotys, two dollars. With this you could buy food for a whole day."

It didn't matter. You became inseparable. Could Mendel have been the reason the kids never teased you or made up mean nicknames because of your crossed eye? There was Shorty and Hunchback in the gang, but you were always respected. Maybe it didn't hurt to have a bad boy for protection.

Mendel's father was strict, but he was also probably too exhausted to notice the shenanigans of kid number eight. Mendel lived recklessly, at least in retail situations. He'd walk through a store, grab something from a shelf, and keep moving. You usually watched in shock, but once you pointed out your displeasure.

"What are you gonna call me?" Mendel yelled. "A crook?"

"You said it already," you shot back. "I have nothing to say."

That was the first of many fights you remember. But you always forgave each other. That's what you do for a friend who's always there.

When you were both eighteen, you needed money to buy a particular pair of shoes. You and the outfits! Mendel dreamed up a solution: You pooled your money and bought a two-wheeled cart, some frosted cookies and candy. You trudged five or six miles out to the farms and traded the goodies for rags and pieces of iron, which you then carted back to the city. Mendel's junkman brother-in-law bought them from you. Soon, you'd raised enough cash to commission a pair of leather shoes from the shoemaker.

One afternoon, as you made your way to the farms, Mendel stopped.

"Wait here for me," he said.

He walked away and you waited. The police drove by, but still no Mendel. Finally, you went home alone. It would take Mendel a while longer. Turns out he'd spied a piece of iron in a field and had gone back to swipe it. A farm worker witnessed the crime and called the cops. Mendel was arrested and spent a month in jail.

Your mother knew how close you'd come to receiving the same punishment. If Mendel had said you were with him when the crime occurred, you would have been arrested, too. We both know he never would have sold you out. In the future, he'd risk his life for you. Still, she forbade you from doing business with him again.

"Did I tell you to steal?" you scolded Mendel after he'd been released. "Whatsa matter with you? Now we can't work together."

You sold the cart and split the proceeds. The next time you worked together your bosses were Nazi guards.

JANUARY 9, 2011

You swore you'd never come here; I have the notes to prove it. Did you know that I wrote down everything you ever said that made me feel something? So that's pretty much *everything* you ever said.

NOTE: He wouldn't go to a nursing home—he thinks it's like a concentration camp. He says he'd kill himself if he got "real frail" and couldn't take care of himself before he'd live in a nursing home.

NOTE: He hates being dependent on anyone, or confined.

NOTE: He'll use pills.

NOTE: He wants to die in his own apartment, in his own room.

NOTE: He'll take the pills rather than go to a nursing home if his good eye goes.

QUOTE: "I can't stand in a nursing home seeing ninety-five- and one-hundred-year-old people who are incontinent."

Oh, my dear. It breaks my heart whenever I see the package of adult diapers beside your dresser. How I wish I could have spared you that indignity.

2007

You were waiting for the Hanukkah miracle when I found the pictures. They were the only ones you'd never shown me, so maybe you wanted to keep them private. But I couldn't help it—you'd asked me to find your checkbook and said it might be in your jacket. I reached into the breast pocket and discovered what you'd pressed over your heart almost every day of your adult life. The worn leather portfolio was the size of a business card. On the right, you'd tucked two pictures of Vera, your best girl: one from the happy days of your relationship, and one from her youth, in which she looks stunning and regal. On the left, you kept photos of your own youth. They were taken very shortly after the war. In both, you've regained weight but your face is still swollen, especially around the eyes, so it looks as if you've been beaten. The smaller photo appears to be a different version of your handsome passport shot. The larger shows you from the waist up. You are wearing a striped concentration camp shirt and matching cap. On the back you wrote your name, a date, and this word: SICK.

EARLY IN THE TWENTY-FIRST CENTURY

You're lucky you had a friendship so rich that it filled your heart for most of your life. I have some friends like that, but most of them live far away from me. I'm light on arm's-reach friends right now.

I've never had trouble like this before. Sure, I got dumped by three girls I'd been devoted to in tenth grade, but as I've gotten older I've learned that most women have been spiritually hacked by other females at some point in their lives. It's like being tenderized: a beating that makes you kinder in the end. But apart from that traumatic rite of passage, my friend life flourished until I became an adult in the suburbs.

People in suburbs are very cliquey. Maybe in cities, too, but I wouldn't know, because I stupidly settled in a lawn-dominated bedroom community with great schools. Suburbs are also very boring. The antidote to being bored and feeling left out is to find a clique of one's own.

David and I started hanging out with the parents of Carrie's preschool friends. These weren't the type of people I'm normally drawn to. Most of them lived in new subdivisions in houses with two-story foyers and pale carpeting. Shoes in the house were bad manners. They displayed no books on their white shelves and never admitted to experiencing emotional pain, but I figured I'd get below the surface eventually. They were friendly and fun, which I thought was enough for the beginning of a friendship. One hosted a Western square-dance party. Another rented a pony for their kid's birthday party.

Then there was the dinner party.

I didn't tell you about it when it happened, but I should have. You would have gotten quite a kick out of this one.

Let's skip right past the part where one woman invited the men to accompany her to the bathroom so she could prove that she hadn't had a boob job. Forget about the other women who pretended to perform fellatio on desserts. To me, that was just immaturity and goofiness, everyone trying to show who could be the bawdiest.

As people started clearing the table, the host turned the lights down and the music up.

"Everybody dance with someone else's husband!" she instructed.

Nope. Not kidding.

So we did, like lambs, because people do what they're told when everyone around them is complying. I ended up chest to chest with a man who lived on a street of couples rumored to engage in spouse swapping. Of course, I didn't believe anyone actually did that.

As we slow-danced, I said, "This is why people think you swing."

"Don't knock it," he said in the creepiest whisper I've ever heard in real life.

There was only one dance, thank God, before the group settled onto living-room couches, each married couple back together. The front of the room was like a stage, so people took to it. You know those gags where one person stands behind another and pretends to be the front person's arms? That happened. A man stood behind a woman who wasn't his wife while she sang a song and he mimed her hand gestures. Before it ended, he put his hand several inches down the front of her pants. On the inside. Everyone laughed except for the man's wife and me.

"We have to get out of here," I said to David.

When the laughter quieted, I announced that we had to leave early to relieve our babysitter.

"She has a dance recital tomorrow morning," I lied.

They all understood. Dance classes are also big in the suburbs.

The next day, I saw one of the culprits on the Little League baseball field. She was sober and bundled in her let's-pretend-we're-rustic barn jacket.

"Wasn't it fun to act like kids again for one night?" she chirped. Yes, she's a chirper.

What? Was this some kind of cover? Maybe they'd made a pact: We'll pretend it was a crazy lark so Sue doesn't realize we all hooked up amid the Play Doh after they left. Or was she serious—had she honestly engaged in that kind of horseplay when she was young and single? Because that's not what we did in my heyday. Never have I ever let a friend, never mind a friend's sex partner, put his hands down my pants. Not even after those college two-for-one happy hours. Either way, her comment confirmed that this wasn't the social group for me.

We tried to enter other gangs. It seemed like a good idea to explore one of the town's private worship groups, called Chavurat. The super-liberal Chavura seemed like a commune, so there was still the possibility of group sex, but we figured the members would at least be more down-to-earth and spiritual. And they may have been, but when we attended one of their events, not one person welcomed us.

The other Chavura we knew about wasn't taking new members, which was just as well. Their earnest discussions about Torah were like parenthetical asides to their real lives, during which they kept busy with infidelity, lying, and workplace ethics violations.

So we stopped searching for a gang. Fortunately, we met friends who weren't wedded to cliques, either. With three couples we could hang out with on a whim, whose kids got along with ours, who we could be our quirky selves with, we had plenty.

Then, we had nothing.

Our two favorite families moved away within months of each other, one to Seattle and one to London, abandoning us in the middle of the Northern Hemisphere. The third friendship dissolved shortly thereafter when the woman broke up with me because I'd canceled a lunch date at the last minute. I took responsibility for disappointing her with my bad manners and apologized an out-of-proportion number of times, but she still insisted on severing the friendship.

"You're a good person," she wrote to me in an e-mail, "but I just can't take this anymore."

I still don't know what "this" was. My Seattle and London girl-friends assured me that I wasn't a bad friend, which left me even more confused. What had I done to this woman?

David and I continued to meet acquaintances for pleasant dinners. I kept in touch with all my old, dear friends who lived far away. I developed new girlfriendships, but not a new best friend. One of the nicest things about our suburb is that when someone gets sick, the community steps in with food. The victim's best friend usually organizes a food chain, with a different family delivering foil pans of lasagna or roast chicken every night. I've long wondered who would organize my food chain if I got breast cancer.

◦

You used to tell people I was your best friend.

"Anything you need I would do for you, and anything I need you would do for me," you explained.

Ours didn't operate like the best friendships I'd had in the past. We bickered. I nagged and you hung up on me. You asked for things and I gave them to you. But I never asked for what you gave me, which was so much harder to secure than sugar cookies and undershirts. You gave me a clique. Its members were nurses and nurses' aides, dying old people and their gray-haired children, a family of big-hearted Odessans. They accepted me so naturally that I didn't even notice I'd landed in a group that let me forget my suburban loneliness.

Does that make you my best friend? Perhaps. For all these years, you've certainly been the steadiest friend I've had.

JANUARY 9, 2011

The nurse with the pretty blue eyes comes in to check on you. She tells me you were fine at bedtime, but the night nurse reported that you talked in your sleep so often that your roommate started yelling at you to shut up. He feels bad about it now, but he didn't know you were so sick. He's not a bad guy. I can't even blame him for getting cranky when you dribble pee on the bathroom floor.

He says all he could decipher of your mumblings was a word that sounded like "stomach," which also sounds like "coming."

The nurse says they thought you were sleeping late. Since you'd had such a disruptive night, they decided not to bother you. When they finally did, you wouldn't wake up.

They called the doctor, who checked you out, covered your mouth with an air pocket, and called me.

I tell her I want to talk to the doctor. It's been years since I saw one of those on this floor. They never replaced your first doctor after she moved back to Ireland, deciding instead to double a colleague's workload.

I don't expect to see him soon, if at all, but he shows up very quickly. I guess this is what you gotta do to get some service around here.

I ask him questions that are impossible to answer.

"It looks like he's struggling to breathe. Can he feel that? Is he suffering?"

He tells me they're giving you oxygen to keep you comfortable. He can add morphine to the order.

Morphine. That's rather serious.

"What happened?" I ask the doctor.

"Congestive heart failure," he says. "Maybe a stroke."

Well, I want to yell, which is it? Pick one.

If he picks one, my thinking goes, you can recover. If it's both, I'm not so sure. But I keep my mouth shut. I don't want to know yet.

May 2009

Dear Mrs. L.,

Today I went to the nursing home to bring Aron his check. Every month for the past sixty years or so the German government has sent him a reparations check. A token to emphasize how very sorry they are for destroying his life and killing nearly everyone he loved. The first one arrived in 1959. It was for $16, he always tells me. Now, depending on the strength of the dollar compared to the deutsch-mark, he gets hundreds. The extra income always helped him live more comfortably, since he earned so little from his hourly-wage jobs, but it also led to a bureaucratic calamity that almost capped him off.

Anyway, the checks are made out to me, though they're only supposed to be addressed to me. The nursing home people were worried that someone in their mail room would lose (or steal?) the checks, so they asked me to have them sent to our house after Aron moved here. But the Germans screwed up and changed both the address *and* the name on the checks to mine. I don't dare try to get that corrected because then he might not get a check at all, and that would make him totally crazy. Those checks mean something profound to him, something much more important than their modest cash value.

I get nervous every time I deposit the checks. Aron tells me to "Go to the skinny one" at his bank. I nod and uh-huh him, but honestly, I never know who he's talking about. As far as I can see, there are no skinny people working in that branch.

A few weeks ago, I pulled up to the side of the bank building to use the drive-through window. The woman behind the glass pushed a button that rolled a drawer out to me. I put the check and the deposit slip in the drawer and she reeled it back in. Then I tensed. What if she asked about the two signatures on the check? Would she ask who I was, which would precipitate a whole treasure hunt to find the power-of-attorney papers? What if she wanted to know why I was getting cash back? Would I have to explain that I needed it to buy three shirts and a belt for him, and to give him some walking-around money? Would she ask me to bring back receipts? Would she call the cops and accuse me of being one of those "helpers" who bilks her wealthy elderly employer out of millions?

I'm much more relaxed when I recognize the teller and she knows our story. I know she won't question my motives.

After he signed the check, I gave him $100. He feels safe when he has a hunk of cash in his pocket, even though there's very little for him to spend it on, and he has an in-house account to draw off of for haircuts and Life Savers. I've told him many times that he's not supposed to have so much cash because somebody could swipe it, but he doesn't care. He's way past caring about their rules. Sometimes if he's too rowdy they threaten to call Security on him.

"What are they gonna do—bring me back to Auschwitz?" he asks.

I give him the money. It's like returning his manhood to him.

All the best,

Sue Resnick

1934—ANOTHER THEORY

Maybe it was being used to hard work that helped you to survive. You were already accustomed to long, hungry days on your feet by the time you became a forced laborer. You'd chosen a line of work that made you sweat.

"The thing is, I didn't like to be a shoemaker and I didn't like to be a tailor," you told me. "I like to be like a bird, you know, outside. A bird that flies. I didn't like to sit and hang down my head. A tailor always has his head down."

Your older brother became a tailor, leaving the inheritance of the family business to you. At fifteen, you started working with your father as a cattle broker, though you must have apprenticed with him earlier than that. You had to do something after dropping out of school following fifth grade. Early every workday, you'd pull your wagon out from the lot behind the apartment building and walk it to the nearby stable. You'd hitch up the horses and ride down to the farms next to your father.

"You ask if they have a cow or calf to sell. Sometime they have, sometime they don't have. Sometime you can buy something through the day and sometime you ride a few hours and buy nothing and come home with nothing."

But there was no food or rest until you finished your farmboy-in-the-city chores. It was your job to milk the family cows, Black and White. It wasn't easy because they were always moving around, threatening to swat you in the face with their tails or kick over the buckets of milk. You needed to sell that milk, just like you needed to sell the collected livestock at the monthly cattle market.

I'm not sure why, given this experience and your charms, you didn't go into sales when you arrived in the United States. I suppose it's hard to become a salesman when you don't have anything of your own to sell. And when you have that accent and those invisible wounds. At least you continued to work with beef, corned though it was.

JANUARY 9, 2011

Lying here like this does not become you.

Come on, Aron, let's see some action. Let's have a day like the one last month, which was more like a hockey fight than a meal. Did you notice how crazy that was? Probably not. Fortunately, I have the play-by-play.

Lieb's in the attack zone when we arrive.

"Pills!" he's shouting. "I need the pills!"

He's showing some aggressive stick handling as he drives the puck toward the goal. It's four o'clock. The Tylenol and Ativan are in his sights.

"Where is she?" he yells, calling for Nurse Noreen.

All the seats are filled in the dining room tonight, folks. Rink rats in pink cardigans and support hose dot the stands. The players are a rough bunch—not a full set of teeth among them. Lieb is backed by right winger Alan, a man curled in on himself like a larva. He's weak of body, as if he has a long-standing neurological disease, but sharp of mind, as if he's not as old as the rest of the team.

Lieb takes a shot on goal.

"Gimme the pills!" he says.

He's angling for a penalty. But Noreen skates in with the medication. *Do you believe in miracles?*

Play continues. There's a face-off at Lieb's table. He sends my husband off sides so he can privately instruct me to bring $200 next time I come. Why does he suddenly need this cash? A bad bet? New brain bucket? No. He wants to take the home-ice advantage by giving the staff Christmas tips.

My husband returns. Menus appear. Tablemate Alan reads the offerings for the evening meal: navy bean soup, macaroni and cheese, stewed tomatoes.

"And orange sherbet," he says, his nose almost touching the paper so he can read it. "That's ice cream."

Lieb and Alan stay in the neutral zone discussing why navy bean soup is called navy bean soup. Suddenly, Sherman approaches with a hip check. He comes from behind and taps Alan's seat with his walker. He wants to sit with Lieb!

"Sherman!" screams Alan. "You don't do that, Sherman! I'll shoot you, Sherman!"

Now the gloves are off. Alan points his gnarled knuckle at Sherman, his hand becoming a pistol. He's high-sticking! He's cross-checking!

Noreen blows the whistle. Timeout!

An aide glides in to redirect Sherman to another table. He's tall and possibly blind, a rookie player who meant no harm. Noreen soothes him.

"It's okay," she says. "Everyone makes mistakes."

She's managed to prevent a line brawl. Surely this roughing means a trip to the penalty box for Alan? But no—Noreen ignores him while he settles himself down with the defense. Lieb watches with admiration. What a turnaround: Alan turns out to be tonight's power forward.

The navy bean soup arrives. Alan devours his. Aron takes a few tentative slurps, then pushes the bowl away.

"It's bitter," he says.

Slap shot.

YOM KIPPUR 2009

You don't celebrate this holiday, at least not outwardly. There are services in your building, of course, and traditional meals before and after the hours of praying, but you refuse to attend. You've only stepped into a synagogue twice since I've known you, both times for me. Once it wasn't even a religious occasion—just a bad oldies concert that we both rolled our eyes through.

This is the holiest day of the Jewish calendar. It's the day when we stand up in temple—for a really long time, particularly for those of us wearing high heels—and confess our sins for the year, before apologizing in person to those we've really screwed over. Who knows how that turns out for people, but according to my *Gates of Repentance* prayer book, God forgives us for everything, albeit with a wink.

"That's okay," God says, cuffing us on the shoulder. "You tried. I'll forgive you again next year, too." She knows we're screw-ups. She knows I can't stop gossiping.

We're also supposed to fast for twenty-four hours on this holiest of holy days. Among many Jews who, like me, follow the wobbly rules of Reform Judaism—which is a big buffet of Jewishness from which you can take a giant scoop of fun holidays like Purim, but leave the tray of kosher untouched—there's always confusion around this ritual. Apparently, the authorities are fuzzy on it, too, so they give multiple explanations:

1. We starve for a day to pay for our sins.

2. We starve for a day to remember those who starve all the time.

3. We starve for a day to remind ourselves that we possess self-control, which can be dredged up when we're faced with forbidden temptations throughout the year.

4. We starve for a day because we're supposed to focus on praying, not eating.

"For Pete's sake," God says. "Can you shut your mouth for one day and pay attention to the book?"

Umm, no. All I could ever think about when I fasted was food. Have you ever watched TV while fasting, God? It's incredible how many cake-mix commercials run in an afternoon.

I fasted all the time when I was a kid. It was expected, and I was a pleaser who always did what was expected. I never fast anymore. The Jews have suffered enough, I tell people if they ask.

You must have fasted when you were a kid.

You grew up religious, like everyone in Zychlin. It wasn't some modern, secular place like Munich, where the Jews tried to blend. Everyone in your village followed the Orthodox rules, meaning no work on Sabbath and every obscure holiday. You wore hats indoors and out, kept kosher, and rushed home before sunset each Friday to start resting, as God had. You once told me that an old man banged on the windows at precisely eighteen minutes before sundown to let the women know it was time to light the candles. But how could he bang on everyone's window at the same time? You must have remembered this wrong. Maybe he banged on a pot within earshot of everyone's window.

You're not so into Judaism anymore. The Nazis wrecked it for you.

"They took womens that were pregnant and babies and killed them all. That's why I won't go to synagogue."

I don't get the connection. Did such horrors happen *in* the synagogue? Or do you think that if the mothers hadn't identified themselves as Jews by going to synagogue they would have lived?

Of course, I asked you to explain. Of course, you wouldn't. There is so much I can never know. But you gave similar reasons for shunning Judaism at home, too.

"I used to believe all of it," you said. "I wouldn't eat if I wasn't wearing a hat. You could get killed! But then the Germans come on Rosh Hashanah and make the rabbi wear his *tallis* and pick up garbage and cut off half his beard. I don't believe it anymore."

I'd never heard this story from you, but it was familiar from photographs and documentaries: The rabbi with the long beard gets shaved and tortured by the men in the black boots, often on a Jewish holiday. I'd seen it several times, but often wondered if it really happened that often or if the depictions were reprints of one event. But I know you haven't been watching Holocaust films or flipping through commemorative books, so it's clearly one of your own memories. Hurting rabbis must have been a common way for the Nazis to introduce themselves to a village. Humiliate the most sacred member of the community—what a sinisterly effective way to show who's boss.

I don't believe in most Jewish customs anymore, either, but I still practice some of them. I host a Break the Fast meal every Yom Kippur. It was a tradition that I'd inherited from cousins after they moved to a condo that didn't fit the crowd, and we moved to a house that did. All the relatives from my father's side of the family show up to end their day of starvation with smoked fish, bagels, and sweet pastries. You'll come to my house for Thanksgiving and even for the Jewish New Year, but not for this.

"It's dark," you said the first time I asked. "I don't like to drive in the dark."

"I'll pick you up."

"Ach, no. There's wrestling on."

"Wrestling? You're gonna watch wrestling on a holiday?"

"It's Goldberg."

You are such an ambivalent Jew. You've tossed the practice of Judaism, yet you embrace a specific professional wrestler simply because he's Jewish. Even now, when you've given up TV so there's no wrestling excuse, you still don't observe Yom Kippur. Then again, what on God's blood-splattered earth would you have to atone for?

FALL 2007—THE LADY AT THE PARTY

The Lady at the Party was supposed to fix everything. I'd met her before but didn't learn until later that she was well placed in several prominent Jewish organizations. All I knew as I spoke to her over cocktails was that she was a good listener when I needed to talk to someone about the trouble I was having trying to keep you safe. I told her about the letter I'd sent to the nursing home, asking them to take you in, and the cold requests for paperwork I received in response.

"That's ridiculous!" she said. "It would be a *shanda* on the Jewish community if we don't help this man."

A *shanda*—the Yiddish word for shame. Exactly what I'd been thinking.

She mentioned that she knew the people who ran the nursing home and that I should call her if I needed help communicating with them.

It was such a nice feeling to believe someone in power had my back. A dangerous feeling, too, because it raised my expectations. If she thought you deserved special treatment, then I was justified in thinking so, too. She gave me permission to hope, which led to all the blunders that followed.

2009—A TYPICAL ATYPICAL DAY

The nursing home smelled like shit.

As usual, you wanted to spend the visit sitting on your plastic chair by the nurses' station. You'd been feeling sick and complaining about all your ailments again, so you hadn't left the floor in a while. They'd been adding and subtracting all kinds of drugs, but you still just sat in that chair and fell asleep. I almost always tried to get you to take a walk; then you refused, and I backed down. But that day I matched your stubbornness. We were either relocating or saying good-bye. Though they keep the place extremely clean, the hallway still usually has that unpleasant nursing home odor of decaying human diluted with cloying cleaning products, which I've learned to avoid by breathing through my mouth as soon as I enter the building. But even that strategy wasn't working. Someone's soiled bedding must have been in a hamper outside one of the rooms.

I got you to sit in the area by the elevators. There's a padded glider there, the kind I nursed my kids on, and it's much more comfortable than the vinyl chairs. Plus, there are always people coming and going, so it's interesting.

You seemed to adjust to the new scene, so I pushed it.

"Let's go to the gift shop."

You used to go every day, and you'd become friendly with the women who run it, but you hadn't been in a couple of weeks. I was craving peanut M&Ms. Surprisingly, you agreed to this part of the field trip, too. It's only about fifty winding yards from your room, but this was major progress. You treated me to the M&Ms, then bought fourteen candy bars for bribes. You give candy bars to the aides who make your bed and the nurse who helps you shave and God knows who else. I've told you that people will help you without being bribed because it's their job, and because they actually like you, but you don't stop. I guess it's an old Birkenau habit. You must have done a lot of figurative palm greasing to survive.

While I was walking around the gift shop pointing out all the things you could get me for my birthday if you were so inclined (old-lady pins, or tissue-box covers needlepointed with Hebrew letters, for example), I saw that you were getting testy with the clerk. You claimed she had given you the wrong change. I automatically assumed she was right. Why do we do this to old people—just assume you're idiots? But you're always right when it comes to numbers. I've seen you add multi-digit numbers and figure percentages in your head. I realized you were right about the change before the clerk did, but you were getting very frustrated. So, naturally, you snapped at me. You can be such a baby. But I get it—I'm the safe one. My kids snap at me, too, when they're angry at someone else. When she finally corrected the error and you calmed down, you bought a hot chocolate, which she doctored with six sugars and five tiny cartons of cream.

I was sure you'd want to sequester yourself back in your room after that uproar, but I thought I'd suggest more adventure anyway.

"Want to drink that in the lobby?" I asked.

You said yes!

A young woman was cleaning the fish tank, which created a lot of watery sounds. When she finished, a man wearing a tie and dress pants started to vacuum. We couldn't hear each other over the noise, so we sat quietly. Then, as soon as the peace returned, you said, "Was a woman, 1937. She was pregnant. Then she miscarried, then she got pregnant again, then she had twins. In my city. And everyone got killed."

What?

It took me a few minutes to fill in the gaps in this story. The woman's name was Yente. Her family owned the creamery where you hung out so you could see the girl you liked. You got over the girl. But you never forgot the pregnant woman or her twins, who couldn't have been much older than five when they died. I bet Yente would be happy to know someone remembers her after all these years.

I told you I had to leave.

"Do you want me to walk you back?"

"Nah, I'll stay here a little," you said.

That meant you felt strong enough to get to your floor by lunchtime all by yourself. Maybe the extra drugs *were* helping

FROM THE DAY THEY SHOWED THAT MOVIE UNTIL TODAY

Maybe I avoided becoming a bat mitzvah for the same reason you now avoid synagogue. If I don't join them, my immature subconscious may have reasoned, I won't get killed with them.

I've been skeptical about Judaism for as long as I can remember. I used to want to drop out, as if it were a softball team, or violin lessons. I took the word *chosen* literally. We are the chosen people and everyone hates us. Who would choose that?

Obviously, I was confused about the concept of *chosen*. Later, I learned that the legend says we don't get to choose, but that God chose us. That sounded nice, being chosen. But what were the perks? Did we get special presents? Did we get to live better lives than everyone else? Umm, no. It turns out that God chose us to set an example for the rest of the world. But an example of what? Enduring slaughter? How much everyone hates the teacher's pet?

In my prepubescent magical-thinking stage, it seemed insane to voluntarily check the Jewish box. Almost as crazy as admitting that you were a Jew to the Nazis. Why, I wondered naively, had the Jews been so honest back then? Why didn't they hold up their hands at the very beginning—way before they had to sew the stars onto their coats—and say, "No, no—you've made a mistake. I'm not Jewish!"

It could have played out like this when the Nazis came knocking.

> *Nazi: "Hi. I'm here to gather up Jews. My organization will starve, hang, and burn them. Can you help me out?"*
> *Jew: "Oh, I'm sorry. No Jews here. Care for a cheeseburger?"*
> *Nazi: "Love to, ma'am, but I'm on the job. You have a nice day, though."*
> *Jew: "You too! Don't work too hard."*

Instead, we got this:

> *Nazi: "Hi. I'm here to gather up Jews. My organization will starve, hang, and burn them. Can you help me out?"*
> *Jew: "Yeah. Let me get my coat."*

I know this is ridiculous reasoning that will get me into a lot of trouble with the serious believers. I also know that most Jews couldn't lie about their religion. They lived in small communities; they'd outed themselves generations earlier. And though many Jews did run, hide, fight, and conceal their identities, you explained to me one day why so many had obeyed the rules instead.

I would ask you really dumb questions during our official interviews at Vera's kitchen table. Or rather, really American questions. Why didn't you tell someone when you were being beaten up? Why didn't you ask for a reason when they told you to move to the ghetto? They are the kind of questions so many of us have asked: *Why did you take it? Why didn't you fight back?*

"Who you gonna tell?" you said. "You tell the army? They take a gun and shoot you on the spot."

Even if men had tried to fight back, you said, they wouldn't have accomplished more than killing a few Germans. The Nazis were much stronger than a bunch of poor Jews.

Besides, anti-Semitism was something to be tolerated, like windy days and itchy socks. Orders to wear yellow armbands and follow curfews didn't come out of nowhere. They were part of a five-thousand-year-long continuum. No one expected it to get *that* bad.

"Jewish people have a terrible habit," you explained. "You can take him to hang him. He sees the rope. But still, in his mind, it's not gonna happen."

What human could have imagined what happened? At the beginning, it just felt like more of the same. Jews didn't ask questions, you told me. Jews were used to doing what they were told. Even you'd been used to taking it since childhood.

The Polish boys teased you as you walked down the street.

"Hey, Jew!" they yelled.

"Yid, go back to Palestine," they hissed.

You pretended you didn't hear them and kept walking. Or you fooled them into leaving you alone. You weren't going to get beat up like your younger brother did the time they took his soccer ball.

One summer afternoon as you were heading to an orchard, you felt a rock fly past your face. You turned and saw two Polish boys with fists full of stones, poised to throw again.

"Do you know how to get to that orchard up the road?" you asked, even though you knew the route.

The boys, whether stunned by your audacity or distracted by your request for help, lowered their arms and proceeded to give you directions. You strolled away with flesh and pride intact.

Big balls, my friend, big balls. Is that the secret to your survival?

Another summer you sat down for dinner in the farmhouse where your family worked. You wore a cap, of course, as all Jews did back then. A head covering signifies respect for God.

"I thought if I take the hat off, maybe I was gonna die. That was in our minds when we were kids."

For non-Jews, wearing a cap in the house was plain rude. The farmer was big on manners.

"Jew, take your hat off," he ordered.

Again, Mr. Balls, you pretended not to hear. You kept the hat on.

"It wasn't too bad, real," you explained, using your version of the word *really*. "It wasn't like here—people with a knife or somebody with a stick."

Just words, rocks, and fists. Nothing strong enough to make people quit the team.

But I had hindsight. I figured as long as I stayed ambivalent about being Jewish, I might not get killed by the Nazis the next time they came. But if I joined them, if I embraced my Jewishness, there would be no escape.

Of course I was afraid of Nazis, despite living safely in 1960s suburbia. It probably started with the jittery black-and-white movies they showed in Sunday school, with the scary narrator who didn't sound like a real man, and the repeated images of backhoes pushing bones into piles. Those led to classic Nazi nightmares. Don't all Jewish kids have those? In mine, the SS troops goose-stepped through my neighborhood toward my house. They were out to kill my family, the only Jews for miles. Only I could save them, but only if I got home in time to warn them before the Nazis got there. I ran and ran, cutting through backyards while the rows of soldiers stayed on the main roads. They always reached my street before I did, but I always woke up before they got to the front door.

It's not as if I encountered egregious anti-Semitism during my childhood. It wasn't too bad, real. My one bad experience happened during sixth grade. A boy threw pennies on the floor in front of me. Then he said something along the lines of: *You Jews love pennies, right? Pick them up!* It was shocking and humiliating and made me feel very unsafe. But karma got him. That year the boys spent much of recess period trying to make each other pass out. I believe the strategy involved breath-holding and spinning in circles. One day Penny Boy took his turn and fell on the asphalt, face-first. He knocked his teeth through his bottom lip. I wasn't an eyewitness to the accident, but I was fortunate enough to see him being led down the hall to the nurse's office. He was crying, as blood (and, hopefully, teeth) dripped down his chin.

But that was it. Maybe nobody bothered me because I grew up in Rhode Island, the birthplace of religious freedom. Roger Williams founded the state after Massachusetts booted him for his belief that people should be able to practice any religion. He welcomed people from all faiths to his new state, an invitation that led to the opening of the first Jewish synagogue in America.

Or maybe people left me alone because they didn't know I was Jewish. I didn't look particularly Semitic, with my straight hair and pale, freckly skin, especially before my nose outgrew my face. Or maybe they knew but didn't care. My hometown of Cranston, Rhode Island, is full of Italian Americans whose culture is like a sister-wife to ours. We all scream at each other a lot and show our love with platters of carb-heavy food. We all value family above mostly everything else. We "all" have dark skin and dark, curly hair. We all leave our places of worship bloated with guilt.

My fantasy as a child was to be an Italian Jew named Toni. Short for Antonia, a name I'd heard on one of my grandmother's soap operas. At the time, I didn't even know Italian Jews actually existed. Such a crossbreed seemed too good to be true, like being able to perform witchcraft by twitching your nose. I didn't know that the word *ghetto* was Italian, and was first used to describe the forced confinement of Jews in Venice. I didn't know that during the Holocaust, Italy was relatively kind to its Jews, refusing to turn them over to Nazis in many cases, and allowing thousands to escape or hide. Things turned nastier after Germany occupied Italy, but still, an estimated 80 percent of Italy's Jews survived the war, more than any other European country except Luxembourg.

All I knew was that if I were Toni, the Italian Jew, I could still enjoy the few things I liked about being Jewish—dressing up as Queen

Esther, singing a song called "Zoom Golly Golly" in Sunday school, inhaling all that perfume the ladies wore with their fancy outfits for High Holiday services—but I'd fit into my community.

Ambivalence means "simultaneous and contradictory attitudes or feelings (as attraction and repulsion) toward an object, person, or action," according to Webster. Let's add religion to that list. Due to my deep and classic ambivalence, besides wanting to wash my Jewishness off, I also spent time painting new layers of it on.

My parents never required me to date only Jewish boys, so I didn't. Yet it was important to me to marry one, so I did. Why, besides loving him personally? So I wouldn't feel so isolated? Because there's safety in numbers?

David is much more comfortable being Jewish than I am. His family didn't eat ham sandwiches and pork chops like mine did. They belonged to a Conservative temple, whose members are less flexible regarding the commandments. So he didn't fight me when I suggested we start keeping kosher.

I'd had a miscarriage, the first of two. Your wife was infertile, so you know about the death of dreams. They grow with sunshiny recklessness, like dandelions, as soon as the pregnancy test flashes yes. By the time someone is sucking the embryonic carcass out of your womb—and you can hear that vacuum even with the forgetting drugs they give you, which don't, by the way, let you forget what that sound means—you already have the fantasy kid grown and married. It's a loss, even if it only thrived in your mind. And when anyone loses anything important, they look for something steady to hold on to. It's one of the reasons organized religion is still hanging around. I grabbed the railing of Judaism after reading a book of poems and prayers written by female rabbis and other believers. Because the words soothed me, I concluded that becoming more observant would soothe me even more.

During this period, my wealthiest friend from high school married an Israeli at a Newport mansion. They served lobster at the reception, and I didn't eat one bite of it because I was keeping Kosher that season.

I read about the healing powers of *mikveh* baths, small indoor pools filled at least partly by water that's "living," such as rainwater or, even better, a continuous trickle from the Dead Sea. Hitting the *mikveh* is the ultimate in starting-fresh rituals. It's regularly done by people converting to Judaism, and by Orthodox women after their monthly periods. In both cases, the bath is supposed to purify the bather. Orthodox couples refrain from any physical contact between the first drop of menstrual blood and the *mikveh* dip, implying to me that the husbands consider their wives dirty for being fertile. Orthodox men *mikveh* before the Sabbath and Jewish holidays, and less-observant Jews use it to purify themselves before and after all kinds of situations, such as big birthdays, cancer treatments, and grief.

That was my objective. I figured I'd have better luck conceiving again if I washed off the residue of the lost dream baby. Because our town is so religious, of course I found a *mikveh* right down the street. I called, made an appointment, and started scrubbing. A big rule of *mikveh*-ing is that you're supposed to be almost inhumanly clean before hopping in, so there's no barrier between you and the water. Barriers include mascara, fingernail grime, that piece of chicken stuck between your teeth, earwax, and whatever's clogging your nostrils. To make sure you didn't miss any toe lint or sleepy seeds, a *mikveh* lady takes a close look at all the nooks. Mine was named Lori.

She was young, though she looked older in her Orthodox garb. A head *shmatte* and giant skirt don't do a gal any favors, which is the point. Lori was not supposed to be sexually appealing to anyone except her husband.

But she was emotionally appealing to me. She was kind and nonjudgmental throughout the awkward experience. Besides being ignorant about most things Jewish, I was naked. But she coached me through the prayer I had to recite before and after immersing (something to do with thanking God for commanding us to do this), and the technicalities of dipping (no body part can touch the wall or floor or air), and she held up a big white sheet while I got in and out of the water to ease my embarrassment. A few days after, she called to see how I was doing. She told me she'd been having miscarriages, too. We hit it off.

She invited me to her home for Shabbat lunch, which was extremely ritualized. Water was poured over hands, multiple breads were blessed multiple times. She told me about her husband's struggle with depression and his quest to make it go away by burrowing under the Torah, which was how they'd become so observant. She even forgave me after I (mistakenly) kissed him good-bye on the cheek, a huge violation of the male/female touching rules. (I'd like to point out that he gave me the cheek when I leaned toward him; how was I supposed to know?)

I thought we were true friends—that despite our differences, we'd stay connected. Then I learned the truth. The whole thing had been a courtship. She'd wanted me to see the light, drink the Kool-Aid, come to the other side. She wanted me to go Hasidic, and when I made it clear that I wasn't interested, she stopped calling me. It turns out I wasn't a friend to her; I was a project.

Ironic, isn't it, that throwing myself closer to observance ricocheted me even further from where I'd started? Lori hurt me. I used that pain to step out of the dance circle and linger at the edges again, where I'd always felt safer.

1939–1941

There were rapes? You never told me this. I found out at the Holocaust Memorial Museum when I listened to one of your townsmen describe your ghetto. He said the Nazis would grab women on the street and drag them into houses and everyone knew what happened. Warfare rapes. Did you know? Were your three younger sisters touched? Maybe that explains why you can barely say their names, and why you always cry when you do. I bet you knew, and that knowledge is preserved inside your mental box of horrors. I know such a box exists because of the way you open and shut its lid. You'll tell certain stories with length and depth, then you'll stop. Abruptly.

"Ach," you respond to a follow-up question after an anecdote, "why you talk?"

And then you wave your hand as if you're actually swatting the box shut.

But those other people from your town who went through the same acid days as you have revealed how bad it got. They told me, in their taped testimonies, about the rapes.

But that's the middle of this part of the story. You preferred to tell me about the beginning, when you were still there.

It crept up on you. First you were simply scared of war, like everyone else in Europe. There was bombing in September of 1939. The streets shook, and people taped up their windows and hid together in cellars. They were afraid to come out, but then the Germans conquered Poland and made them. They banged the drum until all three thousand or so Jews—half the town's population—gathered in the market square. You saw familiar faces atop Nazi uniforms: sugar factory workers who'd been forced to choose sides: SS or bullet. They made you stand there for hours, shooting bullets in the air to enforce quiet while they ransacked the houses and took what they wanted.

Then they rounded up the men and kept them in a church for three days.

Then the farmers posted signs: DON'T BUY FROM JEWS.

Then the SS set curfews. Six a.m. to six p.m., the streets must be Jew-free. One day your father came home a few minutes after six because he'd been at the stable, putting the horses away, and they'd beaten him over the head.

Then they made you tie yellow strips of cloth around your biceps, as if to strap down Jewish might, muscle by muscle.

Then they changed the rule to yellow stars sewn on the front and back of clothing, over the heart, like targets, so they could see you coming and going.

Then they made you paint the word JUDE on your doors.

Then the Pole in the Nazi uniform kicked you in the coccyx with his boot because you weren't pushing your wagon down the street quickly enough, and you didn't make a sound because you knew that if you did, you'd be taken to the police station and whipped.

Then they arrested all the intellectual Poles and Jews and took them someplace and no one saw them again. And your mother, I'm sure, thanked God she'd never been able to educate her children.

Then they formed a Jewish Council—a *Judenrat*—and a police force. They made the baker, Rosenberg, serve as chairman. The doctor was part of it, plus six other men given no choice but to do harm.

Then they took your homes and forced you into a ghetto. First, it was a relatively civilized resettlement, moving you to certain apartments on certain streets on the swampy side of town.

Then they squeezed you closer together, "like sheep," you told me.

Then you had to board up the windows that faced the main street so you couldn't look out.

Then they made you work for free. You cleaned the street and moved rocks around.

Then the German slapped you across the face because you walked past him and took off your hat.

Then the German slapped you across the face because you walked past him and didn't take off your hat.

Then they shoved more people into the ghetto from surrounding towns, so some two-room apartments housed twenty humans. Like sheep.

Then no one except the Jewish police and officials could leave, unless they were assigned to a work detail. Your uncle was one of them. He was your father's brother, but he was only five years older than you. He'd been a tailor; then he'd served in the Polish infantry in the mid-thirties, so they took advantage of all his skills. He sewed uniforms for the Germans and enforced their laws as a cop.

Then people got sick. They were malnourished and caught typhus. The doctor set up a makeshift Red Cross where he and some girls tried to cure them.

Then they turned the synagogue into a warehouse and covered the windows with bricks.

Then Rose, the girl you liked so much, sneaked you some bread.

Then they took your uncle and his wife to the cemetery and made them dig their own graves and shot them.

Then they came into your apartment in the middle of the night and woke you up. It was the summer of 1941. You'd been under attack for two years. You'd been penned into the ghetto for one. They took you and Bill into the darkness without giving you time to say good-bye to your parents or your sisters.

Then you left Zychlin.

Then things got really bad.

JANUARY 9, 2011

The tattoos drive the remembering. All those school programs and museums are nothing compared to the power of the tattoos. People see them on wrinkled arms placing soup cans onto grocery checkout belts. They see them on arms making fists in preparation for routine blood tests. They see them and they remember.

Who will remember once your tattoo is gone? When you die, whether today or some other time, that symbol will be buried with you. The numbers will decompose. You will come unmarked.

Eventually, all the tattooed arms will disappear. Then the forgetting will truly commence.

How would the numbers look on my arm? I could get the same tattoo in the same place. 141324. Whenever people asked what it meant, I could tell them about you. Then they'd remember again. *Oh yeah, they killed Jews once.*

And I'd get to keep you skin-close.

1941

Now I know why you tell me this salami story over and over again. It's the last family story you have. Warped as it is, you must take it out for display whenever you need a reminder of what family felt like.

You and Bill were in a forced labor camp. What were you doing? Building roads? Shoveling coal? Digging fields? All of your "assignments" run together for you, and so, of course, for me, too. But whatever your job at the beginning, you were doing it while suffering from typhus.

We don't have that disease anymore—at least, not in my world. But I looked it up on my computer so I could try to imagine how you felt. It's a bacterial disease spread by body lice and fleas and crowds. They used to call it "jail fever" because of its sprint through places where people are sealed together. It causes weeks of body-boiling temperatures, vomiting, diarrhea, rashes, head and body pain, coughing, and stupor, which explains its name. The word *typhus* comes from the ancient Greek term for "smoky," or "hazy."

It's treatable with antibiotics, which they didn't have for civilians back then, and which they surely wouldn't have given to you if they had. Without treatment, 10 to 60 percent of patients die.

You felt bad.

Then a package arrived from your mother.

What?

This part of the story always stops me. Packages? What was this, summer camp?

Perhaps the Nazis allowed Jews to use the postal service to keep the charade of normalcy going. Work would make you free and all that.

The package contained food, most notably, salami. You couldn't eat that. You were too sick to eat anything, and so was Bill.

"He ate the whole thing!" you remember, always chuckling when you get to this part. "My brother, he'd eat anything."

The food in the package didn't help you, but the package itself did. It was proof that home still existed. Your mother was feeding you, loving you from afar, sending encouragement tied up in string. *Eat up, boys. We'll see you soon.* What a laugh you'd all have about Bill and the salami when that day came.

1998—A TASTE OF CRAZY

Did you save all of your crazy for me? Because that's what it felt like. You packed away all of your emotional damage as if it were a book you'd get around to reading someday, then you led a fairly stable life for fifty years. When I came along, you flipped out.

Okay, it wasn't that direct a consequence. I know aging probably had more to do with your descent than meeting a fellow depression sufferer did. As the decades passed, your emotional defenses broke down like the collagen in your skin. But maybe it helped to know you had someone familiar with the ailment in your life before you fell. I firmly believe that mental illness is a disease of the brain, just like asthma is a disease of the lungs. No one brings it on himself. I even compare mind-related woes to respiratory illnesses. Low-level depression is like a bad cold—sometimes you need medicine, sometimes just time. What I had—postpartum depression—is like pneumonia: acute, but curable with the right course of drugs. Bipolar disease is more like asthma—chronic, but usually controllable if you take the medicine—and schizophrenia is like lung cancer. Catch it early and it might not ruin your life.

I don't know how to characterize what you have. But I know it involves scarring.

The first time it hit you, in August of 1998, I was surprised. I thought with all your laughter and irreverence that you were this incredibly solid, mentally healthy genocide survivor, a happily-ever-after survivor. But no. Vera called to tell me you were in a hospital on the other side of the city and she needed help getting there to visit you. Somehow you'd gotten yourself admitted to the psychiatric wing. I had no idea you'd been seeing a shrink, but one that you referred to as The Rabbi had been monitoring you, and must have decided you needed inpatient help. You were anxious, Vera told me, and had been screaming in your sleep a lot.

I went with her to the hospital and suggested to the staff that you might be suffering from PTSD. I thought it might be helpful if someone spoke to you about your Holocaust experience in addition to filling you with medicine, but no one appreciated my input. I was nobody in your life but some lady who drove some other lady to visit you.

After two weeks of subjecting you to craft projects, they sent you home with a prescription for antianxiety pills. I drove you to a couple of appointments with your psychiatrist, but if he offered counseling, you refused it. He may have convinced you to take antidepressants, which would explain the next four years of relative normalcy.

I use the word *relative* because every once in a while the anxiety would outrun the pills and you'd end up in the emergency room with chest pains. I'd show up and pretend to be your niece so they'd give me some information. After one of your trips to the ER, I spoke to one of the town nurses. She knew you because she came to your building to do blood pressure checks. Blood pressure has long been your favorite hobby. Do you realize how many blood pressure kits I found when I cleaned out your apartment?

"Someone needs to be in charge of his care," she told me.

She was right. I looked around your world for candidates. Vera's daughter certainly cared about you, but I didn't want to suggest the position to her. What if the romance didn't last and Vera faded out of your life, like everyone else had? Your brother lived too far away to be of any practical help, and probably would have declined anyway, based on his reaction later. From what you've told me, you're more like pen pals than family—in touch for years, but not dependent on each other in any way. You didn't know where most of your in-laws lived; they were even older than you, anyway.

I raised my hand to myself. You always joked that you'd adopted me, but now I really wanted to make our connection legal. I lobbied for health-care proxyship despite your objections for quite a while; then, with no explanation as to why you'd changed your mind, you said yes.

The document is four pages long, but essentially it gives me the authority to make your health-care decisions when you can't, and to ask questions about your care when you won't. It also puts in black and white that you don't want to be hooked up to a respirator or have any other artificial prolongation of your life.

We went to your old-fashioned locally owned bank to sign the document in front of a notary. You knew all the women who worked there; the bank was once an important stop on your flirt patrol.

"There's my baby!" you said to a pretty assistant manager. "I had chickens in forty-five weighed more than you."

I thought I was your only baby?

We pulled a couple of witnesses from the lobby, signed our names, watched the manager sign and notarize hers, and became as good as married—at least in the eyes of nurses and doctors.

"This is a one hundred percent kosher paper," you declared.

Less than a year later, I needed all the power it invested.

After we signed next to the X's, I dropped you back at your apartment. Later, I told a friend what I'd done.

"Now you have three aging parents to take care of," she said.

Put that way, the new arrangement sounded like a burden, but I wasn't worried. I owed you whatever you needed because you had given me something no one else ever had: a character test. Or, rather, God has given me a test in the form of you. *Here comes an old man walking toward you and your baby. Will you smile and walk away? Or will you stand and talk, bring him home, put him in your heart? Will you tell the story that his little sisters didn't live to tell, and someday ask your children to keep his memories pulsing? Will you embrace the task or ignore it? This is your test.*

I hope I will pass.

1941

Dear Zelda,

You put the salami in the package and sent it to the boys. Then what? You still had family around you. Mendel and his wife and baby. What were their names? Aron never remembers, or doesn't want to remember, his only niece's name. Your husband and the younger girls. Helen? She was probably gone by then, taken shortly after Aron and Bill, to a different work camp. Maybe they'd all end up together.

Then what?

You know.

I know.

Does Aron?

"I always think what was it like for my family to be told to take your clothes off and get shot," he once said. But that's not what happened, not exactly, so he must not know all of it. Maybe knowing that you're gone is enough, without hearing the details. I found them in a book, which wasn't difficult. It was a pretty big deal what they did to the Zychlin Jews.

Warmly,

Sue

January 9, 2011

Your hands are huge. You're a petite man, but this mitt that I'm holding is giant. I have the rings in my jewelry box to prove it. Shortly after you moved in, you gave me your wedding band. You'd already forced me to take the rest of your collection: the ring with the black stone that looks like it came from a sinister fraternal club; the gold one with the blue stone that a mobster could get away with; and the "emerald," though that's not a ring anymore. When I started to think you wouldn't be around forever, I realized I wanted something more than your summer pajamas in my attic to remember you by. The rings wouldn't fit, so I asked if I could make the emerald one into a necklace.

"You won't lose it?" you asked.

"No, I won't lose it. I'm a grown-up, remember?"

How is it possible that you literally trust me with your life, but you weren't so sure about me and the gems?

It came out nice. Did you know emerald is my birthstone? Not that I think the large chunk of green hanging from a chain around my neck is a real emerald. There's no way you could have afforded it if it were. If anything, it's some kind of synthetic, or a real emerald of the lowest quality. I actually think you got taken by the jewelry store. I think they sold you a ring of glass.

I love it anyway. It's a piece of you close to my heart.

1942

While you labored, slaved, slave-labored, your family waited for the Russians. You told me the Zychlinites thought the Russians would come to the rescue by 1941, but they still hadn't shown up by the end of the year. The worst got worse instead.

In February of 1942, they dragged the Jewish Council, the Jewish police, and hundreds of others into the street. These people would not go to work camps or to gas chambers. They were shot right there instead.

"The police were going wild, gathering together all the Jewish policemen, standing them in a row and murdering them one by one."

Halina Birek Tsinmon remembered this. Did you know her? She got away, too, and put her memories into the Zychlin book. Most of the stories in the book are about the good times, but Halina reported the bad.

"Hilik Zieger, with his last breath, called out 'Yehi Am Yisrael' (May the People of Israel Live). Oberman's wife was sneakily enticed out of her home with the promise that she would be put in contact with her husband, and when she had walked several steps she was shot in the back, and fell to the ground. Oberman's elderly parents suffered the same fate. Only a small child was left from the family. When a neighbor tried to take care of him, she was shot by the Germans. The little one stood crying in the frost. People were afraid to come near him. Alter's brother was also shot.

"From hour to hour the terror increases. The police take groups of Jews to the cemetery, and there they are slaughtered in masses. The blood of the Jews flows in the sewers of the streets outside the ghetto. Dr. Winogran's wife was murdered because they found a large diamond on her hand. She had violated German orders by not surrendering all her jewelry."

Zieger ran the labor office that sent people like you to work. Alter was the baker who led the *Judenrat*. Oberman was the police chief. Were they shot that day, too, or had they already been arrested and hanged in prison? The few reports on record vary. Even Halina's timeline is confusing. The story she told may have happened weeks before the end, or hours. That's the problem with losing all the eyewitnesses. Fact-checking is a bitch.

But does it matter if the killing happened the second week in February or the first in March? It happened. This, too: After the SS shot people like your uncle in the cemetery, they trashed it. Then they carried away the gravestones, carved with Hebrew letters, and used them to build a pigsty at a nearby estate.

The Jews wouldn't need a cemetery in Zychlin anymore. On Purim, when the children should have been parading around town in costumes, and the adults should have been raising glasses to freedom from tyranny, they all got ready to die instead.

The Nazis planned it for that normally joyous day. They took horse-drawn wagons from the farmers you used to pick fruit for. They probably used your father's wagon. They banged the drum one last time and ordered all the remaining Jews into the square. *You're going to work camps,* they lied. Then they loaded them onto the wagons, which took them through the snow to the train station. The trains brought them ninety miles to Chelmno, where for several months a new innovation in efficiency had been under way. Your family most likely arrived at the courtyard of a manor house that had been turned into a reception center. *You're going to work camps,* they lied again, *so clean up.* They led them to the house where they could see TO THE WASHROOM signs, told them to undress, and took the things like pictures and hairbrushes that they'd held onto from their old lives.

But there was no washroom. Instead they were herded down a ramp and into the backs of vans. Fifty or more people were stuffed into each truck. The driver would turn on the gas, climb out of the van, and crawl underneath it so he could thread the exhaust pipe directly into the locked and sealed back chamber. The truck beds filled with gas. The people filled with gas. It took some of them ten minutes to suffocate. It's been written that the guards complained about that. People taking so long to die tend to make a mess, and someone had to clean it. When the screaming stopped, the driver climbed back into the truck and drove it to a mass grave for unloading.

There are no records of all those killed at Chelmno. It was so deadly that of the approximately 49,400 video testimonies that Jewish survivors gave to the USC Shoah Foundation Institute, only 34 mentioned Chelmno. By comparison, Auschwitz is remembered 13,207 times. But not everyone who lived made one of those tapes, including you. So I like to fantasize that your fourteen-year-old sister, Sarah, ran away and lived at least a few more months in the woods, or that your sister-in-law hid with the baby in a Zychlin sewer, and that little girl is alive somewhere, seventy years old now, and still hoping to meet a blood relative like you.

OCTOBER 2010

It happened again today: a reminder that I'm the most ignorant Jew in the room. I was in the dining hall of a mostly Jewish college after a campus tour with Carrie. We'd taken food from the non-kosher side of the cafeteria, but found seats closer to the kosher section. When it was time to leave, I found the tray-return area a few strides from our table. I threw my napkin into a trash can and just as I was about to put my plate on the conveyor belt that brings the dirty stuff to the dishwashers, a food-service guy scolded me.

"You can't put that here!" he said, his tone disgracing me. It took me a few seconds to realize that this was the kosher discard area, and I'd almost mingled non-kosher dishes with kosher ones, a rule I knew but hadn't thought about. I'd almost sullied the entire operation! Who knows what the result would have been: ritual boiling of each plate? Some kind of holy fire pit?

This is one of the main reasons I don't like being Jewish: It makes me feel stupid. I don't read Hebrew, though God actually knows how hard I've tried. Despite dropping out of Hebrew school as a kid, I took adult Hebrew classes when the kids were little, but I sucked at those, too. After fifteen classes, all I'd absorbed was that the Hebrew letters *shin* and *sin* sound different. Or look different. I can't even remember now.

I don't know when to bend during services. Why does everyone else, even my kids, know when to bend their knees and lean forward during which prayer? I just dip quickly for a few beats after everyone else, which is embarrassing. I don't even know what to call the place where we pray anymore. It used to be *temple,* but now I hear it called *shul* or *synagogue* more often. That makes me feel stupid, too. So much about Judaism makes me feel stupid. Who wants to feel that way on a regular basis?

I sometimes consider switching teams. I spent a Sunday morning in a Baptist church, the kind with women in gorgeous hats and men in bow ties. The kind with a sublime choir and lots of collectively hollered *Amens.* The kind whose message is not one of guilt.

"God loves you! Have a great week!" seemed to be the gist of all the prayers. I left feeling praised, blessed—good about myself.

I listen to a Unitarian church service on Sunday-morning radio. It's much quieter than black church, but it's inspiring. The sermons encourage fighting for justice, being a good citizen of the Earth, enjoying life. Judaism tries to convey similar messages, but with so much guilt and fear mixed in, it's hard to hear it all.

My rabbi tells me I shouldn't feel bad about my ignorance. He gave a sermon once that implied that Reform Judaism values following the Golden Rule much more than specific rules. He said you don't have to know Hebrew to be a good Jew. I appreciated the words, which were surely intended to comfort people like me and make us feel more welcomed. But the message didn't cut through my insecurity. I go to services less and less now, but I haven't been able to cancel my membership. Not after what my temple mates did for you.

1941–1943

You walked to the first camp. You, Bill, Mendel, and about twenty other strong young men—although after a year of malnutrition, the strength would have been relative.

The place was called Hardt. At least that's what you told me. The problem with tracking your whereabouts from 1941 to 1945 is that the place names you've given me are different from the place names officially listed in books about labor camps. Or they're not in the books at all, which certainly doesn't mean you weren't there. Turns out that the legend about Nazis being unimpeachable record-keepers is a bit exaggerated.

"Where were you?" I asked early on, when we were only source and reporter. Or pretending to be only that.

You rambled the names, quickly at first, then slowly so I could try to spell them correctly. That wasn't easy. When you said *Tisticle* to identify one camp, and I wrote it out phonetically, I knew I'd never find that in a book.

Part of the problem was that each place went by different names in different languages at the same time. Auschwitz was also Oswiecim. Was *Tisticle* German, Polish, or Yiddish? If it was Yiddish, it could have been spelled ten different ways, so who knows which version got recorded. I tried all the possible spellings (testicle, tstacle, gonad, ball), but still haven't found it listed.

Another problem in mapping your journey was that you could have named the correct town where you slaved, but the reference books named the business that benefited from your labor instead of its location. That's what happened with "Doytch Air," as you pronounced it. The official, incomplete record of your whereabouts, typed up by a different kind of note-taker in 1945, called it "Deutsch Eve." I searched for fourteen years, on and off, for a labor camp with that name and found nothing. I looked in books at the US Holocaust Memorial Museum. I contacted researchers from Yad Vashem. I Googled and Googled and Googled. Finally, after starting all over and visiting the Holocaust Museum's library a second time, I found, in tiny letters in the back of a massive book, these words: *Deutsche Erd.* After flipping around between glossaries and listings, I learned that those words translate to "German Earth and Stonework," and that Jewish slaves worked for such a firm at the time you told me you were at "Doytch Air." Mystery solved.

I haven't been as lucky with most of the others, and it doesn't help that there is no definitive list of all the forced labor camps. There were about 437 in Poland alone.

So we'll go with Hardt as your first location. Your job was to lay tracks. You weren't hauling rails fast enough, so a guard hit you over the head with a stick. It split open the place where your ear attaches to your head. I can still see the ragged white scar when I sit next to you in the nursing home chairs. It bled hard, and that could have been the end of you. The guard could have been inspired by the sight of you holding your bloody head, red running through your hair and your fingers, to hit harder the next time, or just use a gun. But you had a friend who must have been some kind of wilderness expert. He opened his pants and peed on your wound. The bleeding stopped. You couldn't feel your ear for a week or two.

"Good thing I'm not deaf."

So true. Half blind is quite enough.

Every morning they gave you a square of pumpernickel bread. You were supposed to divide it in thirds and make it last the day. But you were so hungry that you ate the whole thing right away. At lunchtime, when you had nothing to eat, the guard who whacked you would plant his fat self in front of you and eat juicy sandwiches.

Hardt must have been where you received the package from home. Bill remembers another Hardt prisoner getting a package from his Christian girlfriend. He was hanged for it, and the rest of you had to watch him swing until he was dead.

And Hardt was also most likely the place where Mendel stole raw potatoes so you could eat, an act of thievery he paid for with a severe beating. Another time, he and Bill crawled under the fence and managed to bring back some bread from a local farm. They didn't get caught that time, but you remembered some other guys who did. They, too, were hanged. So many hangings. They must get tangled in your memories like necklaces locked in a box.

Then you built roads for Deutsche Erd. You may have slept at a forced labor camp called Falenfeld, or one called Weisengrund. Or maybe you were still at Hardt. I hate being imprecise like this, but this is your story so I'm going with your memories. Your job was to clear the woods and mountains so a highway could go through. For about six months, you pushed heavy wheelbarrows until their weight dragged you to the ground. Then you stood and pushed farther.

"It was real rough," you said. "But it was nothing."

I think the farm came next. It was on an estate in a Polish city that the Germans had taken over. For nine months you lived like the king of the slaves. There were a hundred horses, a couple hundred cows, "plenty fields." They actually fed you meat. Whenever a cow or calf died, they let the Jews cook and eat its rotting flesh.

Then they sent you to another labor camp in another Polish town. And when they finished with you there—after two years of being worn down, but proving you were still strong—you hit the big time. Auschwitz.

People talk about concentration camps, but they weren't all the same. Forced labor camps weren't necessarily a death sentence. The Nazis needed you alive to keep the war machine and the businesses that fed it thriving. Death camps, such as Chelmno, had only one purpose. And the others, like Auschwitz-Birkenau, did both—working people to death in Auschwitz and killing them outright the moment they arrived two miles down the road, in Birkenau—though people were also gassed in Auschwitz and worked in Birkenau, so it gets confusing.

On August 27, 1943, they transferred you and 1,025 other men to Auschwitz. They lined you up for selection. Only 10 went to the gas chambers. They led the rest of you to a slower death. Until then, you'd worn filthy civilian clothes. Your skin showed no dark blue. At Auschwitz you got the striped uniform and the tattoo.

They started that day with number 140,721. You stood in line while they branded 603 men before it was your turn. That must have taken hours, depending on how many prisoners wielded tattoo pens. I can tell from the look of your numbers that whoever plunged them into you had been in a great hurry.

You were scared of the hot needle. You pushed Bill, who was always more brave, in front of you. He's still pissed about that, by the way, though when you tell the story you laugh like older brothers have always laughed at their own pranks.

"I knew if he could survive it, I could too," you said with that big smile.

You survived. Those numbers, 141324, have stretched and faded with age. But they will outlive you.

You didn't stay in Auschwitz for long. They loaded you onto a bus and drove you to a new auxiliary camp that had been set up near a coal mine about ten miles away from Auschwitz-Birkenau. The town was called Libiaz. The mine, Janina.

Three hundred of you became coal miners. Crews of ten or twelve would step into a cage and go down into the earth. Poles blasted the coal off the walls and you shoveled it into wagons. You worried that the mine would explode with you in it. You had good reason to be concerned. Exactly six months before you arrived in Auschwitz, a mine explosion killed seventy-four coal miners in Montana. They'd been working longer hours under riskier conditions than usual to support the US war effort, when methane gas and coal dust, which are present in all coal mines, mingled and combusted. The Montanans belonged to a labor union that was trying to keep them safe. I'm certain you didn't.

You didn't have vacations, either. Even the day they chopped an infected boil from your groin they made you join the work crew.

"They cut it open and put a couple of Band-Aids on it," you remembered.

When the Polish coal blaster asked why you were late, you pulled down your pants and showed him. The bandages had fallen off. He crossed himself and told you to sit down and rest. Then he found you another bandage.

Every night after you left the mine, they made you shower. Sometimes you were too tired to wash your hair, but if they found out you'd neglected it, they took you out in the middle of the night and scrubbed you down with powerful hoses.

"If you're smart, you put your head down. When you look straight at it, you can't catch your breath."

You hated it, but you didn't care anymore.

"I didn't think about nothing. I felt tired. When I went down to the coal mine I could hardly walk. I come up and I was just too tired."

It was time to stop.

"I couldn't lift my hands to wipe my face," he said. "I felt like an old man."

You were twenty-three years old.

"I felt like I was a hundred."

You told Bill you had to get out of there.

"I don't care what they do to me," you said.

You asked him to leave with you.

"Where we gonna go?" he asked. "They gonna kill us."

You both knew there was only one possible destination.

"Whenever they were burning people, we smelled it," Bill said. "On Thursdays."

Who asks to be shipped to the gas chambers? People who still had prayers left in them were praying to stay away.

Bill tried to talk you out of it. He remembers it as vividly as you do. He tried to get you to hold on and you tried to get him to quit.

"I'm gonna stay here 'til I can't work no more," he said.

He was eighteen and you were all he had. One day he came back from the mine and you were gone. No wonder he can't completely forgive you.

They didn't take you immediately. A potato shipment got in the way. Every week a truck came to the mine from Auschwitz-Birkenau to drop off food and clothes and to pick up prisoners. That week, the truck was a day late. They couldn't send you to the gas until the potatoes arrived.

When you got off the truck, a prisoner spoke to you.

"You're a lucky man," he said.

One day earlier, the day you were supposed to arrive, there'd been a selection. The prisoner had seen the strong sent to work and the weak—like you—sent to the ovens.

"You missed it by one day," he told you.

They sent you to the camp hospital, but you saw how sick the other patients were and you suddenly weren't so tired anymore.

"I'm fine," you said, selecting yourself for the work side.

THANKSGIVING 1997

That explains your potato worship. The potatoes were magic. Their tardiness saved your life. Did you vow on that day to thank them by eating as many as possible if you ever returned to a proper dinner table?

We'd known each other for more than a year when you and Vera agreed to have Thanksgiving with us. It's not as if you had other options. I don't think Vera's Odessan family celebrated Thanksgiving, at least not in a traditional, all-the-fixin's way, and none of your people had invited you. After your wife died—or possibly before—you'd lost touch with all of her relatives except The Millionaire with the hat. He was a stray, too, not a host, due to the unsettling lack of children on that side of the family. Bill had plenty of offspring, so he probably had a festive get-together. But even if you'd been included, he was too many states away. All you had as a source for turkey was us.

But you didn't want turkey. You called me the day before Thanksgiving as I was chopping, baking, setting, sautéing, whipping, vacuuming, and generally kitchen-maiding myself into exhaustion. You wanted to put in a special order.

"Can you make me a baked potato?" you asked.

I told you I was making mashed, that baked weren't part of the custom, and that there'd be plenty for you to eat.

"I only like the potato," you said. "My stomach."

"What about turkey? That's gentle."

"It's too greasy. Just a plain potato is good."

You're lucky I'm such a sucker for you. I squeezed one potato into the oven beside the turkey roasting pan the next day. And sure enough, except for one dry piece of white meat, that baked potato was all you ate.

Maybe you didn't eat much because you were too busy observing. If each of us has a special talent—mine is parallel parking—yours is accurately assessing a person's character in less than an hour. Later you asked questions about specific relatives: Why is this one so depressed? What makes that one so fidgety? I was amazed that you could pin down quirks and insecurities that had taken me years to identify. And while everyone had been on company behavior, no less.

My children, as children do, accepted you as just one of the other grown-ups. What Carrie thinks of first when I mention you isn't your sad biography, but the night you watched her and her cousins perform a Passover skit in my living room. Somehow, a plastic "plague" frog hit you in the head, a casualty that barely rattled you. It took a few years of regular visits before Carrie noticed that you didn't blend with anyone else in our lives.

"Why are you friends with Aron?" she asked.

I was drying a crystal water glass after you and Vera had gone home after a holiday meal.

Carrie, who was probably eight, sat at the table while I cleaned.

"Because I like him," I told her. "Friends don't have to be the same age as you, you know."

"Why didn't he go to his family's today?"

"He doesn't have a family. He never had any children, and his wife died."

"Oh," she said. "Can I have a piece of bread?"

I was so grateful for her short attention span. I wasn't ready to explain more. I didn't want to tell her all you'd lost, and how, because that would have meant opening that ugly world to her. I dreaded the day she'd add the terms *Kristallnacht* and *Nuremberg* to her vocabulary. She still believed that she was just as valued on Earth as anyone else. How would she stay innocent after learning that civilized people hated Jews enough to burn the old ladies and shoot the mommies and smash the babies' heads against walls?

TERROR, AN OUTLINE

"How's the book?" you ask every once in a while.

Early in our friendship, you agreed to let me write about you. You know I filled steno notebooks and tiny cassette tapes with your stories; even now, you see me scribbling your greatest hits onto the backs of payment envelopes mailed from Germany. But you can't understand why it's taking so long for me to settle you between covers. One reason is that you're radically more than the source of a story to me. The other is that I'm stymied.

"I don't know what to say about you," I answer. It's the truth. I can't write anything conclusive until I figure out why we're together. Some writers say they find the answers by writing their way toward them. But I need to know the last line before I type the first word. We've agreed that no one wants to read a book that's just another Holocaust tale. They've read it before, or seen it in a movie theater. They're tired of it, inured, past being moved. What's another gas chamber, or one more skinny man in stripes? As they say in publishing, it's not fresh.

Your story is so fresh that it burns your throat to speak of it.

You have spit it out in bits, which reminds me how awful it is— both what happened, and what it feels like to remember. You're a yakker.

When you have a story, you tell it over and over. But you leave so much out of this one. Even if I link together every fact you've provided about those ten or so months you spent in Birkenau, I still have only an outline.

Food
They fed you just enough to survive, you said.

"Why kill you if they need you for work?"

At breakfast, there was soup to eat and bread to take for lunch. You'd eat the bread in the morning, so there'd be no lunch. Dinner was more soup with potatoes, never meat.

Once you ate the soup cold and got diarrhea "so terrible I think my intestines gonna come out," and ended up in the camp hospital. After a day, you noticed dead bodies in the beds, "skinny like a finger." You thought the guards had given them coffee laced with poison and they'd all died overnight. You hadn't had any coffee. Though you could barely move, you told them you felt well enough to work again.

"I never grabbed cold soup again."

Clothing and Shelter
You slept in bunkers with beds hinged to the walls, as in submarines, with a thin blanket that never kept you warm and with your wooden-soled shoes under your head like a pillow so no one would steal them. Not that they were great shoes. In the winter, snow stuck to the bottoms and leaked through the tops so you could hardly walk. But if they'd been stolen, you would have been sent to work barefoot.

Work
You walked two miles between Auschwitz and Birkenau every day to work. You had to pass the selection on the way, and saw young men and women without kids on one side, women with children and old people on the other.

"The ones on the first side told they gonna go take a shower. They took all their clothes away and before you look around, ten minutes or so, they were all dead."

You didn't look at the waiting faces because you were too afraid of the guards. Everyone knew what was going on, especially the ones who manned the crematoria and got killed so they wouldn't spread stories. But you couldn't avoid hearing the music.

"There'd be about ten fellows sitting in front of the gas chamber, playing fiddle and other instruments as if they were going dancing."

Your job was to sort bundles that had been taken from new arrivals before they were gassed. The bundles contained clothes, which contained food, especially after the Romanian Jews came in 1944. You figured they must not have known how bad the camps were, because "they'd bring food with them—they thought they were going to a fancy place." You once found salami wrapped in a *tallit*. Then you looked at the sky and saw sparks coming out of the chimneys, "and I knew they burned the people" whose food you had eaten.

You also got food indirectly from the dead because you and others would throw the sorted clothes over the camp fence and the Poles who lived in the neighborhood would toss back bread in exchange.

Women
The female guards were crueler than the men.

"She was holding a vicious dog and threatened to let it attack the Jewish women and children waiting in line," you told me once, without another detail.

But the Jewish women, who worked on a separate side from the "fellows," were fine. You didn't talk to the girls, but you saw them. Their heads were shaved, but as long as they wore their kerchiefs, "they were so nice-looking."

Brutality
You knew what they did to others. When the Germans needed blood for their soldiers, a doctor would take ten- and twelve-year-old boys and girls who arrived at Auschwitz and siphon their blood until they died, you told me.

But they hurt you, too.

They pulled your tooth without any painkiller.

They made you watch another hanging. This time, they hanged three Russian soldiers. One of them spit in the Nazi's face while the rope was around his neck.

They beat you often, Bill said, because you didn't move fast enough.

They took your sight. One day you reached to pick a green tomato and a guard smacked you over the eye with a stick. Since then, you have only seen light and shapes from that side.

I asked you once if you thought about dying every second you were there.

"No," you said. "You don't think."

◦

And that's all you ever gave me about Birkenau. I can look in other places to find details about exactly what people like you wore, drank, smelled, saw. But I only want your stories. It's a gift, maybe, that this is all you remember. Or is it just all you can bear to say out loud?

JANUARY 9, 2011

Gloria just got here. She stopped for a few moments in the hallway to yell at one of the nurses. She can't believe they didn't wake you up for breakfast. If they had, instead of letting you "sleep" in, even though they may not have been able to give you different medical treatment, at least they would have been able to make you more comfortable, and sooner. She's been through this with them before. She knows breakfast is the only meal you eat well, and she makes sure you're there every weekday. She hates when her colleagues don't do the same.

She's wearing the necklace we gave her for Christmas, for the first time. She wants you to see it.

You two have gotten family-close since I hired her to keep you company. You've practically invented your own language, like twins. You speak fragmented Yiddish/English and she speaks fragmented Trinidadian/English, and both of you seem to have an aversion to completing sentences. With my curiously bad sense of hearing, sometimes I have no idea what you're saying to each other.

But I know she's good for us. She keeps you calm. When they were threatening to send you to the loony floor because you were too needy for your regular nurses, she arrived. She's kept you calm ever since, though you do get cranky and panicky whenever she leaves. You'd have her around twenty-four hours a day if you could afford it.

I'm grateful because she's taken the pressure off me. With her filling more of your time, it's okay for me to visit just once a week.

I can't tell how old she is—I don't know anything about her history—but I know she loves you.

Now she's crying. Now she's yelling your name and shaking your leg.

"Aron! Aron! Wake up now, Aron!"

Dachau, 1945 – A Documentary Screenplay

INT. DACHAU INFIRMARY – DAY

Aron lies in a bed, extremely ill. After a forced march and cattle-car transport from Auschwitz to Dachau in the fall of 1944, he worked "in cement" at a Dachau subcamp. As the Americans approached in April 1945, most of the prisoners were sent on another death march. Those too sick were left to die. He has been in Dachau proper for one night. On the morning of April 29, 1945, the day before Hitler commits suicide, he hears gunfire.

ARON

Velkh iz yener? (What is that?)

CUT TO:

EXT. OUTSIDE DACHAU PERIMETER, SAME DAY

SS guards are shooting at American soldiers. Americans shoot back. They have been ordered to take no prisoners. The fires of the crematoria are still burning. After about fifteen minutes, the SS stop shooting and flee.

INMATE

Brooklyn Dodgers! Brooklyn Dodgers!

Gaunt inmates in striped uniforms press against camp gates. They go crazy with cheers, yelling any American words they know. Americans start throwing field rations over the fence to the starved Jews. They empty their pockets of packs of cigarettes, chocolate, and other supplies.

CUT TO:

INT. INFIRMARY

Aron rises and gets himself outside. He sees "little fellows, tall fellows," with faces that look like his own.

ARON

Du a Yid? (You a Jew?)

AMERICAN SOLDIER

Yes.

ARON

Ton du hob shokolad? (You got chocolate?)

Soldier, who speaks Yiddish with an American accent, hands Aron some candy, the first he's eaten in four years. Contrary to some reports, the sudden influx of calories doesn't make him ill. He will not be sent to the field hospital set up days later by Americans.

CUT TO:

INT. SUBSIDIZED ELDERLY APARTMENT BUILDING, KITCHEN TABLE—DAY

> ARON
>
> When you liberated, you feel better.

> SUE
>
> They really gave you chocolate, like in the movies?

> ARON
>
> The Americans—whether Jews or Gentiles—they were the kindest fellows I ever saw in my life. You don't see this from nobody. You don't see it in Poland, in Russia, any nationality. They used to throw candy to everybody, give to everybody, they felt so bad.

Aron looks at his lap and smiles.

> ARON
>
> We were so happy.

CUT TO:

EXT. DACHAU, APRIL 29, 1945

Soldiers search barracks for hiding Nazis. They kill most instantly. Inmates drag some Nazis outside and beat them to death with their hands, and, in at least one case, a shovel. After several hours, the first liberators are replaced by support troops who man the camp until all inmates, including Aron, move on to displaced persons camps.

DACHAU, 1985

Did I ever tell you I was there, forty years and three months after you left? Probably not, because it's embarrassing. Having any emotions besides pity and rage concerning the Holocaust makes me feel slimy, as if the death of eleven million people is a purse that I'm borrowing for a special night out. It doesn't belong to me, unless you believe those people who say it belongs to all Jews, which I don't. I wasn't personally struck by the Holocaust; I cannot claim its scars. Because my grandparents left Russia and Germany decades before it began and let the strings that tied them to Old Country family members fray, I feel no grief for the blood relatives I surely lost. I have no actual connection to the Holocaust, beyond you, but I've always been obsessed with it.

Is it because I'm moody by nature? Or because I read too many novels about kids scraping through the Holocaust when I was young? I loved the poignancy of them, the attempts at revenge, the fact that they made me feel something. The only one I didn't enjoy, I'm sorry to admit, was *The Diary of Anne Frank*. Her perkiness annoyed me. Didn't she want to scream all the time? How could she stay so strong and silent at that age? I guess that's why most people love her: She was heroic in her silence, which I never could have pulled off. I would have whined us out of hiding.

But the abundance of such books doesn't explain why I was attracted to them. Nor does my upbringing; I certainly didn't come from a family that force-fed me banquets of Never Again. I stopped reading genocide novels during high school (I believe I was alternating between Kurt Vonnegut and Danielle Steele at that time), but returned to the subject when I took a Holocaust course during my senior year of college. The professor talked about Elie Wiesel and Primo Levi, about children of survivors and unbombed railroad tracks. I wolfed down these facts like they were buttered popcorn, but every day as I sat in the lecture hall, I jittered with anxiety attacks. This happened to me, back then, whenever I got emotional. It had something to do with trying not to feel anything and having that strategy backfire. Why risk screaming or crying in public when you can stuff those feelings in a box, I subconsciously reasoned? But feelings, as I've told you a hundred times, find a way to get out anyway. You'd think sweating and shitting my way through the semester would have turned me away from the gruesome facts of your life. Nope. It just made me want more.

After graduating, I visited Europe for the first time. I lugged a giant backpack, though I never slept outside, and traveled with different groups of friends over the course of two months. I hitchhiked from Marcé, France, to Barcelona, Spain, with a girlfriend who kept me calm after we noticed the swastika tattoo on one of our drivers' arms. I rented a room from a single mom and her teenage daughter in a Jewish Orthodox neighborhood in London. And while my friends were kissing foreign-tongued boys in Greece, I chose to flirt with extermination instead by visiting Dachau.

I was with a guy named Joe. We stayed in a Munich pension that catered to models on assignment. The breakfast tables and hallways were filled with stunning men and homely women, their unpainted faces as plain and angular as all blank canvases. Still, they were glamorous, and though that made me feel dull, being surrounded by them also made me feel safe. None of them were German.

Joe wanted to explore the city one night, but I refused to leave our room. I told him I felt sick because I couldn't admit that I was too scared to do anything but sleep. I wasn't even sure what I was afraid of, but I hated Munich. More specifically, I hated looking at the Germans who strolled under the enchanting cuckoo clocks and fed tickets into the turnstiles of the stereotypically clean and efficient subway stations and served us sweet beer and sour cabbage wearing lederhosen. Despite Germany's professed regret and guilt, I knew that some of these people still hated Jews. The older ones belonged to the generation that nearly wiped us out. How could their kids not absorb that hatred as they grew up?

I imagined them laughing at us as we paid money the next morning to board a train that would take us to Dachau. Suckas! You're going there *again?* The train was supposedly the only way for us to get to this tourist destination. Why, I wondered, couldn't they provide buses or limos so no one would ever have to ride a train to a concentration camp again? The irony of it seemed too masochistic to be an oversight.

I had trouble breathing during the hour-long ride. I wanted to climb out the wide windows just because they were open. I wanted a drink of water, just because it wasn't forbidden. I couldn't imagine how I would endure the tour of the camp if I felt this anxious before arriving.

The train doors opened and we walked past the chalky-white guard towers and onto the grounds. The sign over the gates still says ARBEIT MACHT FREI, "Work will set you free," in iron letters. A couple of years ago some guys stole the sign over the Auschwitz gate, which says the same thing in a much larger, fancier font. The cops soon found it and jailed at least one of the culprits, whose motives were never clear. He was either a neo-Nazi or a recovering Nazi trying to reform current practitioners of their philosophy. But even before the museum got the sign back, they replaced it with a substitute, which seemed weird to me. I understand the importance of preserving artifacts from the Holocaust and using them to tell the true story, but I couldn't help feeling glad when the sign was down. *Good,* I thought. *Take it.* I'm sick of looking at it, and I'm sure the survivors could live without it, too.

Past the gate there's that wide gravel path that leads to the buildings. It reminded me of a country lane. The air was mild and plentiful. I could breathe. In fact, I didn't feel anxious at all. It was as if by walking into that prison willingly, I'd shaken something loose. I traipsed around the bunkers and the crematorium as if I'd been there a hundred times. My steps were light and bold; I felt impatient to see everything, and lighthearted as I discovered the reconstructed barracks and sterile gas chamber. I was so oblivious to the creepiness of the place that I abandoned Joe at the ovens and took off by myself. But I didn't feel alone at all. And a line kept going through my head like a repeating song lyric. *They can't hurt you anymore,* I thought, over and over. Not: *They can't hurt you* or *They can't hurt you* now. But these exact words: *They can't hurt you* anymore. I knew it was kooky to think these words, but they felt comforting.

On the train ride back to Munich, I relaxed into my seat and watched the pleasant village slide by as we pulled away. Joe, like a normal person, was shaken and tense. I leaned my forehead against the window glass and saw a face. It was a twelve-year-old girl. She was hollow-eyed and silent and I knew she was me. Then an older couple entered the picture. I knew I wasn't really seeing these people, but it didn't feel like the work of my imagination, either. The images were popping up on a screen in my head as if from my subconscious, though I wasn't asleep. The man and the woman, who I knew to be the girl's parents, gave me an order: Go on and live your life.

Because she hadn't be able to.

I never told you this for a few reasons.

1. It's crazy!
2. It seems made-up.
3. It's crazy.

And yet, there are those who believe that people of my generation are the reincarnated souls of Holocaust victims. Maybe I really was there as a twelve-year-old girl, and my vision was one of those other-realm things that never make sense. Maybe the reason we've seemed so familiar to each other from the beginning is that I knew you back then, either at Dachau or before. Your baby sister was close to age twelve the last time you saw her. Her name was Sarah, which just happens to be my Hebrew name. Am I her? Does that explain why you dropped into my life?

No.

That's crazy. That seems made-up.

Jewish-American Provocateurs

David hates when I use the word JAP. He thinks I'm a self-hating Jew. I'm really not. If anything, I'm an other-hating Jew. And I don't even hate the people I'm referring to when I use the abbreviation for Jewish American Princess. I'm just so disappointed in them for personifying clichés. And I'm afraid that they're putting the rest of us in danger.

Think about it. Hitler got away with all of his shit for so long because he convinced ignorant people that the Jews were rich and controlling and deserved to be taken down. Tyrants throughout history have used the moneylender argument to try to get rid of us. I'm not saying it's a correct assessment, of course. Plenty of Jews aren't wealthy. Plenty of flashy people aren't Jews. And plenty of wealthy Jews do the right thing, no matter what the social risk. Most important, no amount of obnoxious behavior or perceived abuse of power justifies genocide. But I'm saying if the anti-Semites insist on continuing the game, we should play a little defense. That means, stop handing them ammunition.

Whenever I see a person who happens to be Jewish flaunting his or her wealth and status, I get pissed. Especially if she's acting like a privileged jerk while doing so. Like the time the woman wearing Chanel sunglasses and carrying a Gucci bag threw a fit in the post office because the clerk couldn't make change for a $100 bill, the only form of payment the customer had with her. Or the time a local temple pushed the gold metaphor too far.

I learned about it in an e-mail that announced, in bold letters and with great excitement, the upcoming gold buyback event to raise money for the congregation.

"With gold at historic highs, this may be the right time to 'cash in,' " the e-mail announced. "Sell your old, broken, and unwanted gold (and silver) jewelry (including broken chains, single earrings, etc.) and receive immediate cash payment."

You have got to be fucking kidding me, I thought.

Nope. It was real. A jeweler would be on hand at the upcoming craft fair to BUY GOLD FOR CASH. He would donate some of his profits to the temple. He would be "paying on the spot."

"Enjoy the craft fair and make real money while you shop!"

And we wonder why they hate us.

My favorite part was the word *unwanted.* Because, you know, we have such an excess of gold that it's starting to block light from coming through the windows.

Would I have been this offended if a church were holding the same fund-raiser? Probably not. I still would have found it tacky for a group to associate such blatant commerce with a place of religion, but not threatening. Non-Jews don't have to worry about being stung by this stereotype. But come on, Jews. A gold fund-raising event? Should we also bring the blood of a Christian neighbor child for matzo baking? How about hiring an artisan to sell knit caps for our horns?

One could argue that letting such things upset me means I believe the stereotypes to be true, which I don't. But I know that other people still believe them. Your family died because their fellow citizens were gullible to stories of Jewish evils.

I know I shouldn't use the term JAP; that gives the bad guys fodder, too. I should just say what I feel: Tone it down.

I'm still scared.

MAY 1945–OCTOBER 1949

And then you seized power for the first and last time. No wonder you remember these years as the greatest of your life.

After the Americans saved you, they sent you to a displaced persons (DP) camp close to Munich. You and refugees from all countries, and of all religions, ate and rested, but you weren't crazy about the setup. You'd heard about a DP camp where almost everyone was Jewish, so you requested a transfer. That got you four years of fun and frolic in Feldafing.

Here's what was so good about it: You were twenty-six years old and got to act it. There was sex and dancing and money earned furtively. You rode the train wherever you wanted. You made payback and love.

Here's what was bad about it, in your mind: nothing.

Yet Feldafing was far from a palace. The one-time Nazi training school was overcrowded. There wasn't enough food or clothing, so former prisoners were still wearing their striped camp uniforms, or they had switched to brown pajamas left behind by the thirteen-year-old schoolboys. Though the guards now spoke English, you were still expected to obey.

It's not surprising that you weren't treated like kings. The attitude from the top was atrocious.

Big shot General George Patton, responding to a famous report on the despicable conditions, wrote in his diary: "[He] and his ilk believe that the Displaced Person is a human being, which he is not, and this applied particularly to the Jews, who are lower than animals."

Nice.

Even Jewish organizations did less than they could have done to help, at least, at the beginning. When an American military rabbi—who made the first stink about DP camp conditions—asked the World Jewish Congress for help reuniting people with their families, the Congress gave him bureaucratic excuses for withholding assistance. I believe this is called foreshadowing.

Eventually, conditions in the DP camp improved. Truckloads of clothing arrived. Schools, theater troupes, and newspapers materialized. Jewish organizations made your well-being a priority, and General Dwight D. Eisenhower himself inspected Feldafing to make sure it was decently habitable.

But you don't remember celebrity visits. You remember teaching another displaced man how to flirt. You remember the big cakes they made every Sunday. You remember having enough money to pay a tailor in the DP camp to make you a black pin-striped suit. You remember teaching people how to dance.

The steps came right back to you. Or maybe they'd never left. Maybe you waltzed in your imagination to get through the hours of emptying dead people's pockets. I'll have to ask you about that when you wake up.

You had always danced in Zychlin.

"Everyone in my family could dance," you said. "Before the war we would walk a few miles to another town. Some fellow would be playing the fiddle. The couples would get up and dance."

Your aunt and uncle were dance instructors, though you don't remember them teaching you. You just figured out how to tango, foxtrot, waltz—all the steps.

"People are born knowing all kinds of things," you said.

I'm a horrible dancer, but I asked you to show me your skills one day. There in your tiny apartment, you jumped up from your chair and held out your tattooed arm. I stood in front of you. You took my hand, put an arm around my waist, and began to count: One, two, three, four, *onetwothreefour*. Your steps were fluid. You held your head high, looked down at me and giggled, becoming for a moment a boy again on a dance floor in Poland. So many bad things had happened since those days, yet your body never forgot how to twirl, how to glide through an imaginary box, and how to sweep a girl off her feet. I wonder how many of the leftover humans in that DP camp remembered how to live again because you taught them the same steps you were trying to teach me. I wonder how many of them wanted to swoon like I did at that moment.

Let's not forget that you got handsome in the middle of these wonder years. A Jewish surgeon at the nearby hospital clipped something behind your eyeball, and just like that, you weren't cross-eyed anymore. The operation cost you nothing except two weeks in a bandage. The new you was even happier than the old you, if that was possible.

"We were living like there was no tomorrow. We didn't know what would happen next."

Love, perhaps?

You met Leah on the dance floor in Feldafing. She had a round face, pretty black hair, and brown eyes. She wasn't too thin or too fat, too tall or too short. Just right, Goldilocks. The band played and you asked her to dance. Then you talked.

She was a few years younger than you, also from Poland, and also alone in the world. You shared stories about what you'd been through. There was chemistry, but no proper place to act on it. You both lived with roommates, but even if you'd had a swinging bachelor pad, you wouldn't have slept with her. She was a nice Jewish girl; you took care of your needs by sleeping with the enemy.

People who plied their prewar trades of making shoes and clothes in the DP camp earned cigarettes and, sometimes, money, but you never got paid for giving dance lessons. It didn't matter, though. The black market kept you flush enough.

You remember the routine. You'd wake up in your own bed in the room you shared with a couple of guys. After breakfast in a cafeteria, you'd head to the train station and take a short ride to the farms or the city. The black market consisted of the Jews trading camp supplies, such as food, cigarettes, clothing, or material, to German farmers for eggs, chicken, or butter that was then sold at a markup back to the Jews or to other Germans. Then you'd take the money you earned and buy more farmers' goods and repeat the cycle.

One farmer, a lady in her seventies, claimed she had nothing to sell you.

"Do you know who I am?" you asked. "I am Jewish. Do you know what happened to the Jews?"

The old lady realized she had something to sell after all.

"What do you want?" she asked.

The next time you visited, she acted like you were best friends. She insisted she hadn't known anything about what the Jews were going through during the war.

"Did you read the paper?" you asked.

But chickens weren't the only things the guilt-ridden Germans gave up. After years of living like a eunuch, you had no trouble shoving a length of fabric or pair of stockings at a girl and convincing her to spread her legs. It must have felt even better emotionally than it did physically. Screwing those girls, back in the day when no one admitted to premarital sex, stole their dignity. A minuscule percentage of the dignity their people stole from you, but still, something.

"I wasn't the only one to be with Germans, even if we hated them. It was almost like revenge, taking advantage of those girls."

The problem with sex, even for revenge-seeking guys, is that sometimes emotions cross the border. Hermanie Holzei was twenty-one when you met her. She was "a little bit plump, blonde, with freckles on the face, blue eyes like Germans." She babysat and cleaned for a couple you knew from Zychlin who'd had a baby in the DP camp. She took you to her family's small farm. If you brought cigarettes or booze for her father, he'd let you sleep in her bedroom.

"Plenty of Germans were poor after the war and let their daughters do the same thing," you told me.

You brought her stockings and other nice things, too, but that's not why she slept with you. You had a connection; you weren't in love with her, like your older brother had been in love with his wife, but you cared about her. Not enough, though, to take her to America when your paperwork came through five months after you met.

"How can you marry somebody who, if not her father, then her grandfather or uncle, used to kill your family? You can't marry somebody like that."

Her mother once warned you not to get her in trouble.

"Don't do something foolish," she said in German.

You two were careful (however people managed to be careful in those days), and Hermanie didn't get pregnant before you left. But I wonder if she may have found out she was pregnant after you were gone. You officially ended the arrangement by mailing back the photographs you'd taken of her. I suspect you neglected to include your new contact information. Imagine the story that would make—learning that you actually had a child in the world. Of course I've been trying to find Hermanie, just in case that's true, and also to ask her what she remembers about you. But it's not easy with the clues you've given me: her first and last names spelled three different ways, the year she was born, a vague memory of the town she lived in ("a ten-minute walk from the Muhldorf station"). But I'll keep trying.

You claim you've never been in love, and that you never regretted leaving Hermanie behind. But Leah—the girl you flirted with when you left Hermanie's bed—stayed in your mind. You should have married her, you realized later, but at the time your low self-esteem spoke louder than your rickety heart. You had no trade, so, in your mind, nothing to offer that sweet girl.

Nothing, perhaps, was yours. But not nobody.

Finding that man was probably the best thing that happened to you during those years of power and joy.

2009

Dear Dunkin' Donuts,

Would you please, please, *please* bring back crullers? Because I have an old man who's jonesing bad for crullers, and I am spending way too much time looking for his fix. They used to be standard, right there beside the jelly-filled and the honey-dipped donuts. Then you got rid of them because they were too time-consuming to make. Come on—you have time to invent something called a sausage pancake bite, but no time to twist a cruller?

I've tried appeasing my man with supermarket crullers, but he just leaves them in the bag to harden. He's even accused me of purposely bringing him stale pastry.

It's challenging enough to keep up with his endless requests for new electric razors, belts that fit, fresh undershirts, Pepperidge Farm sugar cookies without green sprinkles, and the goddamn coffee cake he used to buy. But now I have to go from store to store, looking for crullers that taste like yours. Have some mercy.

I love your business. I love the smooth simplicity of your coffee. I love that I know I'm home when I arrive at Logan Airport because it smells like Dunkin' coffee. I love the invention of Munchkins. I just don't love this bullshit with the crullers.

Bring 'em back. It would improve at least two people's lives.

Sincerely,

Susan Kushner Resnick

1945

You knew in your heart that Bill was still living. And you were just as certain that he thought you were dead.

"He knows when they sent me to Birkenau, I can't still be alive."

I'm sure you gave your names to the officials trying to plug families back together, but you made the connection before they could. You were yakking with a couple of guys who'd come to Feldafing from a DP camp a couple hours away. You mentioned your brother and they instantly recognized the name of one of their soccer mates.

"He is with us!" they said.

You hopped on a train to go find your little brother. When he saw you, he thought he was seeing a ghost.

"I figured maybe he just got up from the ground and came up to me," Bill told me.

After you had vanished with the potato shipment, Bill stayed at the coal mine until the war was almost over. He managed to stick with your old friend Mendel the whole time. The Nazis marched them. For two weeks, they starved and froze and stood straight as people dropped dead around them. As the Allies approached, the Nazis forced them into open cattle cars that went back and forth between locations. When the Americans finally liberated them, they sent Bill to a hospital. After three months there, he went to a mainly Polish DP camp. When you found him, he was living in a private apartment with a roommate. You stayed for a day, though he remembers it as a week. He also remembers a slightly different version of how you found him. His involves soccer players meeting you on a train, thinking you looked familiar, and asking if you'd had a brother in the camps. But the *how* of the reunion never mattered, just the reunion itself. For the rest of your time in Europe, you took trains across Germany to visit each other. For the rest of your lives, despite many disagreements, you haven't let go of each other.

You tried to find the rest of your family, too. The most direct way was to go back home.

You went with Mendel. As the two of you walked across the bridge that led to the city, Mendel asked a man if there were any Jews around. The man told him "there were so many Jews, plenty Jews." But when you got to Zychlin, there were only four Jewish people remaining. One of them was a shoemaker who'd married a Polish girl. The other three would come back to Germany with you.

You couldn't believe they were the only ones left out of the thousands of Jews who'd once lived in Zychlin. You went to the house near the synagogue where your aunt and uncle had lived. The windows in the house and in the synagogue were smashed. You went to the creamery where your first crush had worked. The sign with their name still hung on an outside wall, but the house was closed up tight. You even went down to the cellar where the girl had kept the cottage cheese and the cream, but it was empty. All the Jewish houses were empty.

Your final stop was your family's last apartment before the ghetto. You knocked on the door of the apartment owned by the lady who had lived across the hall. She was still there. She told you that one day your older brother had knocked on the same door. He was crying and told her that the next day they were all being sent away. Was he looking for refuge? If so, she didn't give it. She just watched as the Nazis forced her neighbors onto trucks headed for Chelmno.

You left Zychlin. You left Poland. And lucky for me, you left Europe, too.

MARCH 2010

We have to make appointments to prove you're still alive. Every year the Germans have mailed one of us—you when you managed your life, me now—an envelope containing a piece of paper titled *Lebensbescheinigung*. That cumbersome word means "Certificate of Life." The form is very basic. It asks for your name, birth date, marital status, naturalization and social security numbers, and signature, and it asks you to circle some words—"*am Leben ist* / is alive." I might not technically have to circle them, but I do because I don't want them to forget.

The Germans require us to fill out this form so they can continue to pay you back for what they took from you. Not that that's actually possible.

"If they gave each one a million dollars, it wouldn't make up for what they did," you said once.

Amen to that, Brother.

But they won't take our word for it. We have to get the form notarized. We used to go to the bank, but now I have to make an appointment with a lady in the nursing home's marketing office. She's very nice, though she lightly scolded me the one time I didn't schedule in advance.

This year it was an ordeal to get you to her office, which is right outside your hallway. You'd stopped leaving the hall, and sometimes you refused to leave your room. I worried that even though I told you we were going to visit this lady, you'd be sitting around in your pajamas. It had been a pajama kind of month.

But you were ready for a day of business, blazer and all.

We shuffled down the hall and waited for the notary. There wasn't any place for you to sit, which was a little inconvenient since you were worn out from the walk, but you leaned against the counter and your walker. The notary took out a box that held her stamp and embossing seal as if they were jewels. This was really quite a ceremony. She watched as you trembled your name onto the paper, then she banged and pressed her fancy tools, and just like that, our government proved to their government that you were still living.

A Chart

European Jews to Israel 1946–1951: 380,000

European Jews to the United States 1946–1950: 105,000

Of those, the number that spent time in a concentration camp: 20,400

Israeli Holocaust survivors estimated to be alive in 2011: 208,000

American survivors estimated to be alive in 2011: unknown

There is a shocking lack of accurate data on US survivors. I wanted to find out how many people who'd been through the worst of the worst, like you, had made it to the age of ninety and beyond. But it was impossible, partly because survivors aren't divided by severity of treatment (anyone who faced hardship in a Nazi-occupied country qualifies as a survivor), and partly because no one has taken a count in more than ten years.

FALL 1949

You wanted to go to Israel, but the spots on your lungs held up the process. While you waited, a relative in America found you. Your great-aunt, sister of your grandmother, sent you an invitation to the States. At about the same time, Hadassah connected you with one of your father's friends, a man I'll call Chaim Pitler. That might have even been his name. Or, it could have been Pitl or Pittel, which you've also told me. You and the Yiddish transliterations are driving me nuts. This man had moved to Washington, D.C., before the war, and had built up a chain of bakeries. His invitation included a job, so you took it.

"I was told there was so much money in America they were sweeping it up on the street!"

They gave you a smallpox vaccination and sent you to my Promised Land. You puked for seven days on the boat to New York. When you got off, you had a small Hersey bar in one pocket and Pitler's phone number in the other. The Hadassah people who met you dockside gave you $3 and a train ticket to D.C.

Pitler was supposed to meet you at Union Station, but he wasn't there. And like so many greenhorns, you had to find someone in the train station who spoke Yiddish and beseech him to call the number on your scrap of paper.

After one night in Pitler's house, he took you to his main bakery and showed you how to fry and sugar the donuts. He helped you get a social security card. He taught you to use the bus.

The bus rituals were weird. Why, you wondered, did you get to sit in the front of the bus, but the black people had to walk to the back? You'd only been in town for one day. It didn't seem fair.

Then Pitler suggested you get your own apartment. Maybe he and his young wife, who was closer to your age than his, wanted their privacy back. Or maybe they couldn't take your screaming at night. You dreamt about your family in the early years, especially your father. You'd be walking together and a soldier would come up behind you, jab a rifle into his back, and order, "Go! Go!" You'd wake up covered in sweat.

You found an apartment above the bakery. The landlord asked you to pay for the rent in advance. You'd never heard of such a system.

"Advance?" you said to Pitler. "What am I, a whore?"

The biggest problem with D.C. was that you couldn't find people who spoke Yiddish. You were lonely. After a couple of months, you decided to start again. Pitler put you back on the train, this time headed north. Your great-aunt and cousin met you at the train station and brought you to their Massachusetts home, where you officially began to live your version of the American dream.

PRAYERS

We've established that I'd never win any Mrs. Jewish America competitions, but sometimes I don't mind going to services. I can make it fun. When the rabbi asks us to pray silently while standing, then sit when we're done, Max and I have a contest to see who can stand the longest. I have been known to wait out the entire congregation. And I like reading ahead in the prayer book when things get boring. I've noticed that when they're not bossing you around and guilting you, those pages offer some great wisdom. I especially like the Meditations, which are printed before the meat of the services and usually skipped.

I found this line attributed to Holocaust survivor Rabbi Leo Baeck: "When we are approached by a human being demanding his right, we cannot replace definite ethical action by mere vague goodwill."

And this bit from Deuteronomy: "Do not harden your heart or shut your hand against the poor, your kin."

And together we say, *Aaaaa-men.*

1942

Helen, the sister you bickered with the most, made it out of Zychlin before the final roundup. They took her for slave labor, just like you and Bill, during the summer of '41. She was nineteen, the same age my daughter is as I write this. While you picked up rocks and rails, she picked up food she wasn't allowed to eat. The Nazis sent Zychlin's able-bodied women to farms and fields. Helen bent and crouched every day as she pulled potatoes out of dirt and twisted tomatoes from vines. Other vegetables, too. Did she sneak a bite now and then, a risk that surely would have resulted in death? Perhaps not. When they brought her to Auschwitz, she stood in the selection line with her friends from home. In a different place and time, girls like them would have been standing in lines waiting for a bouncer to decide if they were well-dressed enough to enter a dance club. Cute girls would help the business thrive. In Auschwitz in 1942, the bouncer decided whether they had enough color in their cheeks and meat on their bones to enter the barracks. Strong girls would help the business thrive.

They put a girl Helen had grown up with on one side. They put her on the other. The girlfriend lives in Brooklyn.

Helen was only twenty.

FALL 2007

There was a man you wanted me to call. You opened your pink address book and pointed to the name. Arnold.

"Who?"

"Arnold!" you yelled. "Mendel's son."

Mendel had a son? Mendel, concocter of schemes, stealer of iron, had a conventional life after the war?

Not exactly. First, he continued to scheme and steal.

While living in the DP camp, he worked the black market as you did. But he either went further or wasn't as careful. From what you remember, he used counterfeit ration cards that he'd gotten from a gun dealer to buy butter at a legitimate shop. The owner called the police and Mendel ran to an apartment building and hid under the stairs. But the cops found him and a judge threw him in jail.

"I'm a Holocaust survivor," Mendel appealed. "I've been imprisoned for four years."

"Now it will be four years and six months," the judge declared.

When all the displaced persons were scattering, he chose to go to Israel. He served in the army, met his Czechoslovakian wife, and had two children, a girl and a boy. They sent you a picture of the kids, the big girl holding the baby, with the words THE FRIENDS OF ARON scripted on the back. You got to see them in person when the family moved to the Bronx in 1959. Mendel got a job painting houses. You remembered that he used to call you long distance from his customers' phones.

You visited him whenever possible—as often as once a month, you said. His wife was a good cook and you loved his kids. Arnold remembers that you'd give them five or ten bucks whenever you saw them. His sister said you and Mendel were like brothers. She remembers even deeper generosity: When the family had financial trouble during their early years in the United States, you gave them money out of your deli-counter wages and Holocaust reparations to help them get by.

When the kids grew up, Mendel's daughter moved back to Israel and convinced her parents to join her in 1984. You visited them and still talked on the phone, but the time between contacts grew longer by the year. That's what happens when friends move to a different part of the world, as I well know.

It had been years since you'd spoken to Arnold, who'd moved to California with the military and stayed for a career with the postal service. After you gave me his number, I called and arranged for him to call my cell phone at a specific time while you were living at a temporary nursing home. We sat in the hallway and I handed you the tiny phone.

"Hellooo!" you said to Arnold.

Then a smile. The conversation must have brought you back to those nights around his kitchen table, when you were a welcome part of a family. You seemed relaxed and in control for the first time in a long while. Arnold told you that his mother had died that fall, and you said you were sorry, that she was a good woman. Arnold didn't tell you what a rough father Mendel was; that he told him little about his wartime experiences, but played out his rage often.

In fact, you didn't talk about Mendel at all as I sat next to you in that hallway. He had died two years earlier, at age eighty-five, having outrun death for more than sixty years.

1950—Boy Meets Girl

Your marriage was the opposite of a storybook romance. It was another of your tragedies, another area where you got ripped off by life. But I'm not sure you and your low self-esteem see it that way. So I'm giving you this memory as an outsider sees it.

Once upon a time, a lonely man finished his workday washing floors and clearing dishes at a Boston deli. He took the trolley to the next town and entered a room full of people from the Old Country. They were all Holocaust survivors who met to talk about getting settled in America and collecting reparations from Germany. The meetings comforted the man because everyone spoke Yiddish.

On this night, an American girl joined the group. She spoke Yiddish, too. She'd come to the meeting to find a man. Though she was a talented pianist from a comfortable family, she was very overweight. At twenty-five, she still had no prospects for marriage. Her name was Bibi.

She and the lonely man talked that night and exchanged phone numbers at the end. She began to help him. Living with his aunt wasn't working out well because she wanted him to pay rent and she expected him to bring home free food from the deli. Bibi found him a room to rent for $7 a week. It was close to her house in Roxbury, a hot spot for Boston's Jews.

Her father owned a nice restaurant called Speigel's. He hired the lonely man and put him behind the take-out counter. The man knew enough English to fill an order for a cup of coffee and a roll. But when someone asked for a cup of java and a bun, he was confused. Bibi's father gave him other jobs until he learned more words.

The man didn't love Bibi and she most likely didn't love him. The gossips said she spent time with a married Gentile man who was the real object of her affection. But the lonely man liked her parents and they liked him. Her father promised to set him up in business if he married Bibi. He liked that Bibi was smart. It seemed like a good-enough compromise.

They got married in late September. A rabbi performed the ceremony, and twenty guests, including the man's great-aunt and cousin, attended. He wanted to wear the suit he'd had made in the DP camp, but Bibi wouldn't allow it. The man loved that suit; it didn't even wrinkle in the rain. But she made him give it away. She loaned him the money to buy a new one and made him pay her back every month. It was a sharp suit: double-breasted dove gray with wide lapels. He wore it with a matching hat and a sky-blue tie patterned with a funky sprinkling of rectangles. He weighed 137 pounds, but looked happy on his wedding day. She wore a dark green dress, weighed considerably more, and looked annoyed.

They honeymooned in New York, at the Victoria Hotel. It was a short honeymoon in all ways. As soon as the newlyweds came home, things got bad. Bibi's father sold the business he had promised the man. Bibi spent more money than he earned at his new deli job. They couldn't get pregnant. The doctor said the lonely man's sperm were fine, but that his wife's tubes were closed. She could have had an operation to open them, but because of her weight and her diabetes, the doctor couldn't guarantee success. The man wanted children, but he didn't push too hard. Bibi refused the operation.

They couldn't afford to adopt. No one would ever know what kind of father he would have been: cruel and angry, like another survivor he'd heard about, or tender and delighted, like he was with other people's children?

There weren't many kids around to remind them of what they were missing. Bibi's brother had a couple, but neither of her older sisters had children, the eldest having lost one in infancy.

The lonely man and Bibi began to fight all the time. They moved from apartment to apartment, usually together, but sometimes apart. He had a temper and she was strong-willed. She continued to see other men. He worked ten hours a day, six days a week. On his days off, he'd often take the train to New York to visit his best friend from childhood, or his brother.

He could have stayed there. His brother offered to get him a job at the car upholstery business where he worked, but the lonely man worried that he wasn't strong enough to pull out car seats all day. And he didn't really want to leave Bibi.

"Good, bad, I come home, she is there. A meal is there. I had somebody. If you're divorced, you have nobody," he said.

He couldn't go back to having nobody.

Everyone talked about their awful marriage. They were schizophrenic with all their on-again, off-again nonsense, one of their brothers-in-law said. They were like oil and water, said another.

When the lonely man became a citizen in 1954, Bibi asked him to change their last name. Libfrajnd was too hard to spell. She chose Lieb and told him it meant love.

The Liebs went to dinner with other couples once in a while, or to the park with her parents on summer afternoons. They went to New York together sometimes, and ate Jewish food on Delancey Street. Bibi didn't dance, but the man missed it. Twice he went to dance halls by himself, spinning with women he knew but sitting by himself between numbers.

Bibi graduated from community college when she was in her fifties. Wherever he lived, the man hung the photo of her receiving her diploma. She worked at a hospital as a medical transcriber, and eventually she was promoted to head cashier. She lost almost one hundred pounds early in their marriage, but gained it all back. He was frustrated because she didn't take care of herself. The doctor said she was "digging her grave with her teeth."

He almost left her twice. He was tired of the fighting. "I say day, she says night," he told people. The first time he took off, thirty-five years into their marriage, a girl was involved. He bought a one-way plane ticket to Israel. He'd been invited by a woman he'd known in the DP camps. Back then, she had married a different survivor from Zychlin, the man's hometown. After her first husband died, the woman wrote to the lonely man. She wanted him to divorce Bibi and marry her. He packed his bag and went to the airport in Boston, but the flight was canceled due to storms. He was supposed to return to the airport the next day, but he got scared and stayed home. The other woman married somebody else a few months later.

The lonely man still wanted to get away from Bibi. Later that year, he tried again. This time he was serious. He mailed all his winter clothes to his brother for storage. He boarded a plane, even though he hated to fly, and made it to Israeli soil. He stayed with his childhood best friend, but felt unwelcome. They fought. He didn't know Hebrew, so he felt as isolated as when he'd arrived in America. He had a talk with himself.

"I am real foolish. In the United States, I know everything. Here, I'm sixty-five years old and I can't order a cup of coffee."

He flew back home. He'd only been gone for a week.

He nursed Bibi through the last years of her life. When she lost a leg to diabetes, he pushed her wheelchair. When she couldn't wipe her butt, he did it for her. He dressed her and cooked for her. Her sisters, who were quite well-off, didn't come to help. One of them even stopped taking Bibi's calls, saying they were too upsetting. When Bibi died at age sixty-six, the man didn't invite anyone to the funeral. Because of how her family had neglected her, he thought he'd feel like a hypocrite if he welcomed them at the end. It was just the funeral home guy and him at the graveside.

The next day, he was lonely all over again.

JANUARY 9, 2011

Your Timex sits on the night table. This must be one of the first days since the war that you haven't worn a watch.

I have spent almost as much time shopping for watches as I have picking out new electric razors for you. Without these two items in perfect condition, you get rattled. But you're not easy to please. When you first asked for a new watch, I bought you a nice one with a metal strap and shiny roman numerals from a jewelry store. You sent it back. Then I exchanged that for a digital with a stretchy band. You sent that back, too. It took me a while to realize that what you really wanted was an analog watch with large, clear numbers and a leather band. It took me even longer to find that simple watches like that don't seem to exist anymore. Except at Wal-Mart, where I found exactly what you'd asked for in the spinning Timex display. You were thrilled.

Now I understand why. I'm reading a book about Feldafing, your displaced persons camp. The author, a man who lived there himself, noticed that by the winter of 1945, most of the DPs had acquired watches.

"Feldafingers wear watches all the way up their arms, so that they can be seen easily by all," Simon Schochet wrote. "They are highly-polished and pampered, much like the pets of the idle and lonely."

He thought it was strange to see "undernourished and poorly-clothed" people almost obsessively fiddling with and talking about their watches. But he understood it.

"For the former prisoners, a watch was proof of being a person of worth once again. For them, after years of deprivation, a watch represented all that was civilized and comfortable in the modern world."

Watches, like Holocaust survivors, are becoming more memory than reality now. People use their cell phones and computers to tell the time. Not me, though. I look at my wrist and see that it is close to noon. You've already missed breakfast, so you must have lunch. It's time to get up now.

1950–1981

After your father-in-law sold the place he'd promised to give you, you found a job on your own. Blue Hill Avenue was Main Street USA for Boston's Jews, and Jewish delis were its town halls. One of the well-known joints was called Jack and Harold's. You worked there as a counterman for ten years, one week of the 4:00 p.m. to 12:00 midnight shift followed by a week of the 6:00 a.m. to 4:00 p.m. day shift, like a coal miner.

But Jack and Harold's was like a farm team compared to the most famous deli of them all: the G & G. You took up an apron there in 1963, the year I was born. It was a big place, with about 250 seats that opened at 5:00 a.m. and closed at 1:00 a.m., seven days a week. Contractors came in the mornings to hire day workers, as if it was a union hall. Families broke their Sabbath hibernation with Saturday-night dinners there. College kids, cops, couples, even residents of the local mental hospital—everyone came to the G & G for all the classic Jewish foods: bagels and cream cheese, gefilte fish, chicken soup, brisket, tongue, and, most famously, corned beef sandwiches, which, of course, you didn't eat, being partial to well-done roast beef or grilled cheese sandwiches on your breaks.

Besides being the center of the Jewish community, the G & G had been a political hot spot since Roosevelt stopped by during his 1932 presidential campaign. When Vice President Hubert Humphrey made an appearance in 1964, 20,000 people crowded the streets around the deli to see him. Jack and Teddy Kennedy made requisite G & G stops, with Teddy assembling sandwiches during his Senate campaign. And Boston and state politicians would end their campaigns with final speeches at the G & G the night before Election Day. They'd stand on tables or on a platform set up under the neon G & G sign and make their final pleas for the Jewish vote. The most famous Jewish politician at the time, State Representative Julius Ansel, spent so much time at your deli that he had its phone number printed on his business cards.

The place was such a big deal that it was immortalized by an artist on the walls of your Jewish nursing home. When we first toured this place, you were delighted to see a painted version of yourself in the white counterman's apron and cap you wore every workday.

The owner, Ben Klingsberg (the first G had died, and he bought out the second one), loved you, and, more important, he trusted you. He gave you the keys to the store and let you make the bank deposits at the end of the day. You'd come in before the pre-daybreak opening to set up. It was on one of those mornings that you cut an onion roll and your hand at the same time, requiring stitches and a week off. It was the only vacation you remember taking.

Then the neighborhood began to change, thanks to an ugly bank and real estate scheme that lured black families to the area and scared off Jews. As the Jews ran away from their new neighbors, they took their deli orders with them. The most famous deli of all closed in 1968.

You were the only employee Klingsberg took when he opened a new restaurant in a fancier part of Boston. Called the Eatwell Cafeteria—way too cutesy a name for a real deli, I think—it catered to office workers and was only open on weekdays. When the businesses supplying those customers moved out of the city, Mr. Klingsberg followed. He took you with him when he opened a place in the suburbs, but it was never anything like the G & G. You sliced your last block of meat when it closed in 1981.

1994

You were supposed to keep the German money in a separate account so the US government wouldn't touch it. Our country had reasons to feel guilty, too. Not bombing the tracks. Turning the *St. Louis* away. This was our way of trying to make amends.

You earned it, we said to the survivors. *Enjoy!*

The Victims of Nazi Persecution Act of 1994 states that "payments made to individuals because of their status as victims of Nazi persecution shall be disregarded in determining eligibility for, and the amount of, benefits or services to be provided under any federal or federally assisted program which provides benefits or services based, in whole or in part, on need."

Congressman (and, presumably, nice Jewish boy) Henry Waxman introduced the bill after hearing that one of his survivor constituents was having trouble paying for her subsidized apartment. The government had counted her reparations as regular income when they raised her rent. Now she couldn't afford it.

"In the aftermath of World War II, the postwar German and Austrian Governments instituted programs of payments to Holocaust survivors," Waxman said on the House floor. "These payments are not intended to be full and adequate compensation for the Holocaust, as such compensation is impossible. They are instead a penitent gesture to individuals whose whole families were exterminated, who suffered loss of limb or permanent impairment of mental or physical functions, or who endured other terrible hardships. It is unconscionable that these payments should count as regular income or assets, thus diminishing eligibility for aid under entitlement programs of the Government of the United States."

Besides, he pointed out, there weren't many of you left. The extra expense to the country wouldn't last for long.

His fellow Congress folk agreed that taking torture amends wasn't very nice. The House and Senate passed the bill, and President Clinton signed it into law.

No one told you to celebrate by opening a new bank account.

MAY 2002

I'm still not sure you understand the concept of psychosomatic illness, so here's Webster's best definition:

"Of, relating to, involving, or concerned with bodily symptoms caused by mental or emotional disturbance."

It doesn't mean, as many people believe, that the sickness is imaginary, as in *It's all in your head*. It means the pain is real, but it originates from your brain rather than from a physical injury or germ. You had been displaying classic symptoms all spring. Something would make you anxious and the anxiety felt like a heart attack, so you'd call 911. Because you uttered those hysteria-inciting words—*chest pain*—the doctors usually kept you for observation. They never found anything out of the ordinary, which frustrated everyone.

"What's wrong with me?" you asked. You called me from your hospital room. It was your third admission of the spring.

"Maybe it's stress," I said.

"You sound like the doctor," you said angrily.

"Well, we kind of agree on that."

Click. Dial tone.

You hung up on me.

It wasn't the first time, though it surprised me whenever you did it. So dramatic! We've always bickered, which still delights me. It's freeing to have a friend like that. I usually try to restore peace so the relationship doesn't get messy. But I'm not afraid I'll lose you if I fight back.

"Do I have to go over there?" I asked David.

"Yes," he said. "You signed up for this. You're responsible for him. He needs you."

People have asked what my family thinks of you taking up so much space in my life. I think they expect reports of resentment or annoyance. But that has never happened. David adores you, and often walks around the house doing a perfect imitation of your voice and accent. My kids see you as my project—just something Mom does. And I think they liked to be able to say, when they were learning about the Holocaust in school, "My mom is friends with a *real* survivor." Basically, they see me as the family do-gooder. Nag, neatnik, and do-gooder.

Still, you're my gig. So, you hang up and I come running. Isn't such negative reinforcement supposed to backfire?

Your nurse, who had brightly colored Batman and Spiderman tattoos on his giant biceps, told me the doctor suspected an anxiety problem. They were trying to get you to take antidepressants, but you were resistant.

You were asleep when I entered the room. You had a white face-cloth on your forehead, and your striped pajamas were open to reveal electrodes on your chest. Nobody had changed the bloody gauze pad taped to your forearm.

You opened your eyes and gave me a sweet, soft smile. Then you took my hand.

"Listen to me," you said. "In concentration camp, when a man has a big stomach they say it's because he ate too much. I know I have this pressure in my chest."

You were referring to a good-looking Greek man you used to say hello to in Birkenau. One day, you noticed he was bloated from starvation, which killed him a few days later. The guards had insisted he was distended from overeating. You thought the doctors and I were twisting the truth the same way the guards had.

We argued about it some more. You insisted you had nothing to be depressed about, and I tried to explain psychology to you. I'm sure there was some bed-pounding and eye-rolling involved.

"Just take the pills," I said. "If they don't help, you can say you were right."

Your hospital room had a big window that overlooked a factory roof and the town hall. The sky was still blue, but the sun was nudging the horizon. I'd never turned the lights on when I arrived.

"You look nice in the dark," you said.

A nurse came in and silently checked your blood pressure and pulse rate. I expected us to continue the fight after she left, but instead you ended it. You agreed to take the pills. This time, I took your hand.

"Why are your hands so warm?" you asked. "They're usually cold."

JULY 2002

The pills either weren't strong enough to beat down your anxiety or they came too late. You continued to drive yourself and everyone around you crazy. When you were admitted to a hospital, you flirted with the nurses and charmed the doctors. When you went home, you obsessed about your health and called 911. If you were in a hospital bed on a day when your social security or reparation checks were supposed to arrive, you'd hound me to go to your apartment, pick them up, bring them to you to sign, and then drive immediately to the bank to deposit them. If I tried to tell you the checks could wait a few days, you flipped out and yelled at me, which certainly wasn't helping you recover. You wanted me to pay your bills, too, which required more runs from my house to your house to the hospital to the post office. Eventually, the ladies at the bank suggested I take on power of attorney duties so I could handle your finances. We signed more papers. Now I could take control of your death and your taxes.

A few hospitalizations later, the doctors—and probably the insurance company—decided you belonged back in the loony bin. This time they found you a room in the geriatric psych ward of your usual hospital. It was after dark when they finished the transfer paperwork. They made me walk you to your new wing.

I was relieved because I thought this transfer meant you'd finally get the treatment you needed. Like the last time, they'd patch you up good as new. Then I saw your room.

It was straight out of *One Flew Over the Cuckoo's Nest*: tiny and starch-white, with furniture made of metal and windows reinforced with chicken wire. The door locked from the outside. It was a cell.

We both started to panic. You didn't want me to leave, but you were too proud to ask me to stay. I knew you weren't actually a prisoner and that no one would hurt you, but that room was awful. I wanted to get you back to the floor we'd come from. The nurses behind the secured front desk couldn't help. It was too late at night to undo a transfer. And for what? You still needed psychiatric treatment. They told me they'd keep an eye on you and would call if you needed me. I had to believe them.

I helped you get ready for bed, then promised you'd be safe. *Just sleep*, I told you. *I'll make sure you get out of here in the morning.* When I left, you were sitting on the bed. I've never felt like more of a traitor than I did the moment I closed that door. Some best friend, huh?

I didn't sleep much and went back as soon as I'd dropped the kids at school the next morning. I expected you to be furious with me, but you weren't. You had made it through the night. You actually seemed okay.

I think you realized before I did that you were in the right place. The psychiatrist assigned to you was a Russian woman who wore hip blue-rimmed glasses. She understood your past, she got the PTSD component, and she was smart enough to prescribe a cocktail of pills that actually did patch you up. She also figured out why you seemed to thrive when you had nurses to answer your calls and aides to bring you trays of food.

"Sometimes it's just time to let people take care of you," she said.

She thought you were ready for a nursing home then. But you weren't.

When you were discharged a couple of weeks later, we met you in the hospital lobby. I had Max with me, and though he was standing next to me instead of cooing from a baby seat, the scene reminded me of the day we'd met five years earlier: the same three people in a lobby, unsure of what would come next.

2010

You want to die in your sleep, but you thought that could be risky.

"Who checks the heart?" you asked me not long ago.

"Huh?"

"The heart. Who checks it?"

"When?"

"At the end. Before they bury."

Oh, I see. You wanted to make sure they didn't mix up *asleep* with *dead* and bury you alive by mistake. Throughout all our pre-mortem conversations, I don't think this had ever come up.

I assured you, I think, that the doctors followed special protocols to prevent the burial of living beings. The funeral home guys, too. And me.

"I will make sure you're not still alive," I vowed.

SOUL MATES

Plato explained the concept of soul mates by having Aristophanes recount a famous myth in his book, *The Symposium*. According to the myth, Zeus split humans in half to keep us from getting uppity. Ever since, we've been searching for our other halves so we can feel complete. Most people think of their soul mate as their romantic ideal. I think that's both narrow-minded and dangerous. I once dated someone who was very similar to me. At first it was wonderful because we love ourselves, right? Then it turned disastrous. Because we were so similar, we made the same mistakes. There was no counterbalance— no one to pull us back by the belt loops when we got too close to the edge. In a pairing of opposites, there's always someone to see how crazy you're getting and yank you back.

Put another way, when you're with someone who's just like you, you get more of the same. With an opposite, you get all kinds of things you've never had before.

Vera is your opposite and David is mine. We've compared notes on this. We were in one of those hospitals on one of those summer nights when you were unraveling. I told you I understood how you felt because I'd been anxious for years before postpartum depression forced me to get treated and allowed me to become a recovering nutcase. You hadn't made peace with your weaknesses yet.

"Nothing bothers Vera," you said.

"Same with David," I said.

"Good thing we have them because we're both nervous."

You looked at me and laughed. I realized in that moment how similar we are. And so many times since then I've known how you will react to something and you've known how I feel about another thing. We look at the world in the same cynical way. We laugh at the same things. Does that make us soul mates—two halves of the same person?

Is that why you picked me up—so that during this brief period in both of our lives, we get to feel whole?

January 9, 2011

I wonder if we would have had so much trouble getting you into this place if The Millionaire was still alive. I like to think that he would have fixed everything with one check—that he would have done the right thing. But I think that about everyone, don't I? And I'm usually disappointed.

He was married to your wife's sister, the one who lost the baby. They never had any other kids. I don't know how he built his tower of money, but I have an idea how he maintained its height. Rich people get rich because they make money, but some stay rich because they keep it. He may have been good at that.

You remembered his lack of generosity when you asked if you could buy two cemetery plots from his family's section so your wife could be buried near her sister. He charged you $700 for them, which you didn't think was right. Poor people like you often get pissed when their wealthy relatives don't cut them breaks. How would a family discount have hurt his bottom line, you wondered?

I visited him once, with your permission. His house, in an upscale section of an upscale town, wasn't huge or terribly flashy, but I could still tell he was loaded. He cultivated orchids, for God's sake. And he had live-in help.

I tried not to look at him while he spoke because his eyes disgusted me. Gravity had dragged his lower lids so far down that the bloody insides showed. I get queasy when I look closely at bloodshot eyes. His made me want to puke. But avoiding them wasn't a problem because he didn't look at me much either. Not the friendliest sort.

He told me that when your wives were alive, you'd see each other on holidays. Everyone gathered for Passover Seders at your mother-in-law's house. After the women died, you two stayed in touch. You'd meet for lunch at the pancake house. He said you had a "native instinct," whatever that means.

"He's a hard worker and a good human being," he said.

When he died at age ninety-seven, all he left to you was a hat. You knew he had a bunch of nieces and nephews, but still—a hat? At least it was a quality hat: forest-green velour decorated with a green satin cord that always reminded me of a yodeling costume. It came from the Swiss men's clothing store, Fein-Kaller, a place that had been selling fancy clothes to fancy men since 1895. Someone from that institution embossed The Millionaire's initials onto the inner lining of the hat in gold letters. You mocked him for only bequeathing you a stupid hat, but you loved that hat. You wore it whenever you got dressed up, even if you weren't leaving the building.

Then it disappeared. You asked everyone around you to look for it. You asked me, continuously, to search my attic in case I'd stored it with your off-season clothes. All of us complied because we knew how important that hat was to you. It was your only valuable possession and your last link to your American family. The rest of them abandoned you after Bibi died, or maybe they thought you had pushed them away by not including them in her funeral. In any case, they've been replaced by a warmhearted family of Russians, and by me and mine.

2002—THE GOOD NEW DAYS

"You've gained eight pounds," the doctor said.

I'd brought you in for a routine checkup shortly after you'd left the mental hospital. The doctor held his stethoscope over your sleeve-less T-shirt and listened. He heard strength. He looked at you and saw spryness. Then he had to eat crow.

"You and the rabbi tell me I'm eighty-two years old and you can't do nothing. Over there, in the hospital, a woman, a little Russian woman, she gives me the medicine to make me better. I feel, not a hundred percent, but when I get the chest pain, I put a heating pad on and it goes away in half an hour."

The doctor's face was blank. He wasn't going to admit that he'd failed to fix you.

But I'm sure I was smiling. Whenever you emerged from your depressions, I felt like the parent of a wayward child who has gotten back on his feet. I could finally let out my breath.

You'd moved into your own single apartment by then, in the same building as Vera's. You still ate your meals and slept most nights at her place, which I know because you once told me I could sleep in your bed, "if you ever have a fight with your baby." I don't think the building manager would have allowed you to share her apartment, and your stuff wouldn't have fit anyway, which was just as well. You liked having a place where you could be surrounded by your records, your framed pictures of the old days, and a coffee table that your late wife had hand-tiled.

We had our best moments in that apartment. One day, I sat on the stained carpet looking at your record collection. Johnny Mathis, Tony Bennett, an album of JFK speeches, and lots of Sinatra. He was your favorite, though you never told me which song of his you liked the best. Mine has always been "In the Wee Small Hours of the Morning."

I asked you the tough questions in that apartment, the things I wanted to know before you died.

Me: How long do you think you'll live?
You: 'Til I die.
Me: Why do you think you're still here?
You: To keep an eye on you.
Me: Do you believe in heaven?
You: Who the hell knows?

Me: I think there's heaven.
You: See, you afraid to die. Who says there's heaven, the rabbis?

I told you we needed a plan so you could let me know if heaven exists. You nodded.

Me: What will the signal be? How will I know if you're there?
You: When you dream about me.

And one winter afternoon when it was already dark at 4:30, you handed me a brown paper bag in that apartment. The bag, soft with wear, was full of photographs and documents. You and Mendel after the war. You and your wife's family celebrating a holiday. You patting your father-in-law's cheeks after you'd shaved him. You and Bill in New York. Your naturalization papers. The mug shot that proved you were alive again.

"Don't you want these?" I asked.

"Nah," you said, flapping the idea away. "What do I need with them?"

The better question would have been: What do *I* need with them? But I didn't ask that, of course. I was grateful and a little scared. I'd never been given custody of someone's memories before.

SPRING 1969

Purim was my favorite holiday, too, but that shouldn't surprise either of us. Not if we believe we're two halves of Zeus's whole.

My adoration of Purim is evident in the picture my father took of me sitting in the backseat of our station wagon. It's morning and we're about to leave for Sunday school. I must be about seven, and I am dressed in a regal gown. Okay, maybe not regal, but long and hand-stitched and definitely the color of buttercups. I'm also wearing a tiara, because what else would Queen Esther wear on her head? It's the absolute best day of the religious school year because we're required to dress up as Purim characters. I am delighted with my getup, as evidenced by my giant front-tooth-free smile. This is almost a fluke. I didn't give smiles away like some kids do. They had to be earned, which may explain why in most of my childhood photos I look pensive, except for the ones that show me crying. My parents liked to load up the camera when I was in tears. There I am crying in our play fort over a meatball sandwich they insisted I finish. There I am crying while wearing an adorable bonnet. But tears weren't a factor in the Purim photo shoot. Queen Esther's eyes were dancing.

Costumes weren't the only good part of Purim. In my day, unlike yours, there weren't house-to-house shenanigans, but we got to go crazy during the annual retelling of the Purim story. We were encouraged to wave *groggers,* handheld metal toys that growled when spun, and make whatever other noises we wanted—*even in temple*—whenever Haman's name was read as a way to symbolically blot him out.

I wonder if hundreds of years from now they'll read the story of the Holocaust during services and encourage the children to shake *groggers* whenever they hear the name Hitler?

FALL 2006

You called me from an emergency room. *Oh crap,* I thought. *Not again.* I rushed over. This time they'd taken you to a hospital in a rougher neighborhood, the kind where gunshot cases are routine. When I found you behind a curtain, you looked like one of them. Blood covered one side of your face and had dripped all over your shirt.

"What happened?"

"The lamp. I stood up and cracked my head."

The covering on this floor lamp was glass. You must have moved your kitchen chair too close to it. Later, when I went to clean up the blood, I saw that you had split that solid glass in half. Talk about hardheaded.

They'd already sewn you up when I arrived. They said I could take you home, which was a relief. I didn't want to leave you in that scary place. But the bigger relief was that for once your problem was simple enough to be fixed with a needle and thread.

JANUARY 9, 2011

The doctor said it could be a day or two before anything changes. You know I'm not very patient, but I can wait. Surprised? I know—I'm usually running in and out of here to get to the next task on my list. But I'm all yours today; I have no errands or kid duties planned. I have no fireworks to watch.

That was years ago. We were sitting in the dark, the only light coming from the hallway, you in the bed, me in the chair on your left. Of course this was in an emergency room. I honestly don't remember the complaint that time. It was usually chest pains, though you switched it up sometimes by insisting you'd had a stroke.

What I do remember is the pull. It was the Fourth of July, and for a change we had plans. We'd been invited to a party at someone's lake house. This was a big event that we'd never been included in before, and I'd been looking forward to it for weeks. The kids and David were already there, waiting for me. And you didn't want to be alone.

I was in a state, as my mother used to say. I couldn't decide which of my actions would be more selfish: staying with you and abandoning my family, or going to them and abandoning you?

Max was six years old. What if he got scared of the fireworks and needed me, both for comfort and to hide him from braver friends? What if Carrie didn't know anyone at the gathering and wanted to leave so she didn't feel left out? I am their mother. They are my priority. Besides, I wanted to be with my family, which is a different kind of selfishness.

But there you were, alone in an ER bed, thinking you were close to death. We were waiting for the doctor to bring in test results. I knew I shouldn't leave before the results came in. What if this time you were actually sick and needed me to make a decision? What if you freaked out and they ignored you?

We waited as the sky got darker, the fireworks nearer. Finally, the doctor whipped open the curtain, reading the file as he walked. Nothing serious, he said, but they'd admit you for observation. I knew it could be hours before they got you into a room, but I also knew you were okay.

I dashed from the hospital to the party, though you didn't approve my exit. I couldn't even find my kids at first, because they were busy having fun without me. Clearly, I'd dreamt up their neediness. I found David and tried to have fun, but all I did was worry about you alone in the ER. As soon as the sky filled with smoke from the final firework, I dashed back to the hospital. You were asleep in a single room.

No one had really needed me after all. I'd just driven myself crazy for nothing. This is a hazard for those of us continually trying to prove that we're good. To whom, or for what? Impossible to know. There isn't a shrink with a sharp-enough knife to dig that deep.

As the kids got stronger and you got weaker, prioritizing became easier. When you had a crisis, you came first and they understood. When they needed structure and routine—i.e., basic mothering—they came first and you didn't always understand. You'd look at me with contempt when I cut a visit short so I could pick one of them up at school. It was as if they were fully capable adults and you were the child. Today, though, don't worry; they will understand if I stay until after the stars come out.

2006

Vera was your world. She was the timber that held up your roof, the legs on your table. When she suffered a series of strokes, you began to tilt, too. But not right away.

First, as you have so many times, you started a new family. This one was a sort of boys club. Every day you and two other men met at McDonald's for lunch.

I don't know how you met them, but probably the same way you've met everyone important in your life: by talking to strangers. They were nice guys, though clearly more middle-class than you'd ever been. The one who'd served in World War II sometimes brought his wife. The other, a former ad man, had lost his "bride" a few years earlier and still looked terribly lonely. The thing I liked best about them was that they put up with your weirdness.

You brought your own lunch to McDonald's. On the day you invited me to meet the guys, you carried a pink reusable bag that looked like something hospitals give to new mothers for diaper storage. You pulled out of it a bruised pear; two plums; a sandwich consisting of a roll, a slice of cheese, and a leaf of lettuce; and a knife, all of them wrapped in paper napkins. You also pulled out a packet of Nescafé.

"Their coffee's too strong," you said, pointing at the golden arches.

But the McDonald's boiled water was apparently acceptable, because part of your routine involved purchasing a cup of it for thirty-seven cents. The employees offered to give you the water for free, but you refused handouts.

After lunch, you would drive across the shopping plaza to the supermarket, where the pharmacists and the manager and probably every attractive female employee knew you by name. Then you'd go home to watch *Judge Judy*, cook your own dinner, walk down the hall to do your laundry, and visit Vera. That was hard. She couldn't speak much at all, and she was never alone. Her daughter and various aides took care of her night and day. You'd written her daughter a check to help pay for the aides, but that was about all you could do.

Except tilt. Until one day you couldn't hold yourself up any longer.

JANUARY 9, 2011

I should have just paid them. I should have put aside my guilt about barely contributing any money to my family's expenses and asked David if we could use a hunk of our college or retirement savings to pay for your care. He would have said yes, right? He's the nice one.

But I didn't bring it up until we were deep in the shit. For most of that awful year, I was under a spell of naiveté. I really thought they'd rescue us. I thought managing your life and fighting your battles was enough of a contribution from me. I thought we all stuck together.

More practically, I didn't know how much the final amount would be, as you'll see, or that I was allowed to front you the money. I was blinded by the high walls of a bureaucratic maze and couldn't see the possibility of a relatively simple solution. But maybe it's better that it worked out the way it did. How else would I have learned what it takes to be a good Jew?

I gave you the outlines of the saga while it was happening, but not the details. You were in no condition for details. Maybe you aren't today, either.

But you should know all of it. Every good Jew should.

OCTOBER 2007

Dear Zelda,

He sits in his apartment, all alone, with a dingy washcloth on top of his head. It's a shining summer day, but his shades and windows are closed as if it's a dark January afternoon. He wears flannel pajama pants and a stained sleeveless undershirt. I can't tell when he last showered.

You taught him how to cloak his pain this way when he was a little boy with big headaches. A damp piece of fabric, you told him, would make the hurt go away. You would soak it in a bowl of water and drape it over his soft hair. He still remembers. He's still listening to you. But he needs so much more right now.

He says he's going to kill himself. Swallow pills. Use a gun, even though I don't think he owns one. Something just to make the pain stop. His chest hurts all the time, although many doctors in many hospitals have looked all around that organ and found nothing to explain the pain. No heart attacks. No blockages. Sometimes he has high blood pressure. He knows this because he wraps a Velcro cuff around his arm several times a day—or hour, depending on how panicky he's feeling—and takes a reading. If it's too high for too long, or if the chest pain is unbearable, he calls 911. He's sure he's dying.

The emergency medical technicians stop playing cards or making chili or whatever they do in fire stations when nothing's going on, which is the usual state of affairs in our dull town. They pull on their jackets and drive down Main Street to his apartment complex.

It's only a five-minute ride, but it annoys them. They think he's a pest. *Frequent flyer,* they call him, because he phones so often. Sometimes they scold him for wasting their time. Sometimes he shoots back: "Do you think I want to feel like this?"

When they deliver him to the hospital, his blood pressure floats back down to normal. Because then he's not alone. He can't bear to be alone.

The best woman he knew moved out of the building and into a nursing home in the spring. That could be what started this. Perhaps we're all given a finite share of the ability to withstand discomfort, to tolerate fear and pain and endings. And because he used so much of his allotment during the war and because he's lived for so long, maybe he's tapped out. He can't push through one more challenge.

If he calls me before he calls for an ambulance, I can sometimes talk him down. I tell him to drink some tea. I tell him to watch TV, because I know he's sitting in silence, soap operas and wrestling no longer worth the effort. I tell him to go to the lobby and sit with his neighbors, but he refuses. As we talk, he keeps testing his blood pressure. When it steadies, we get off the phone. But if I'm not home when the panic rises—or if he's tired of my redundant advice—he dials 911 again.

I figured getting him into a nursing home would be easy. I thought that when he needed help, the Jewish community would flock to him, lift him up, and take him to the most comfortable, nurturing place that exists in our world. This mecca for ailing elderly Jews was funded in large part by the big spenders in the Jewish community, at least according to the plaques all over its lobby. I figured that those rich folks and the giant organizations they also fund—organizations that throw around slogans like *No Place for Hate* and *Facing History* and the ubiquitous *Never Again*—would have a contingency fund and special sanctuary for a man who symbolized all that they claim to fight for. I figured that although I'd been able to handle his issues for quite a while by myself, they would step in to help both of us when the time came.

The time came.
There was no special place.
There was no special money.
There were very few special people.
Never again, my ass.

Love,
Sue

SUMMER 2007

All the nuttiness you'd ever displayed became magnified. This time, you wouldn't bounce back after a night in the hospital. Your doctor said you needed companionship, possibly an assisted-living facility, but not yet a nursing home. You were still driving, still shopping and cooking for yourself on good days. On the bad days, you'd sit in your apartment with the heating pad over your chest. Your primary food groups were rice and pills. The only indication that blood still flowed through you was the *Victoria's Secret* catalog on your coffee table. But I knew your depression was fixable. We'd been here before.

I talked with your doctor about increasing your antidepressants. He agreed that you needed a medication adjustment, but he wanted you to see a psychiatrist first.

"You always telling me to go to the shrink," you said to him one day in his examining room. "Like the shrink will take me to the moon."

Then you turned to me.

"If I didn't go cuckoo in the camps, I'm not going to."

That was your way of saying no.

Just get out of your apartment, we both said. Eat dinner in the community dining room of your building once in a while.

Again, no.

I started calling agencies. Maybe we could get someone to cook for you. Maybe there was an elderly day-care program that would ease you back into the general population. Maybe you'd eat Meals on Wheels.

"It's dog food," you said after the first delivery.

I looked at one of the disposable plates of brown goo that you had left on your counter and couldn't argue.

The doctor increased your pill dosages. Nothing. He threw new pills at you, stuff for pain and anxiety and heart attacks and sleeplessness. Nothing.

I called people who never called me back. I called people who required paperwork before they would tell me they couldn't help you. Someone sent me a list of housekeepers, but they needed a financial report before they could figure out a fee. Someone else gave me the name of an agency that could help with Medicaid paperwork. The "help" that the volunteer offered was given in the form of a reprimand. She told me to read the forms.

"You can read, can't you?" she said.

"Yes, I can read," I said. Then I hung up on her, just like I'd learned from you. It really does feel good.

The doctor got sick of both of us. He suggested you pour brandy into your coffee. That old-school medicine only turned you nostalgic. You called to instruct me to engrave your tombstone with my name, David's name, and the phrase "best friends of Aron."

I called the Jewish family service organization and they connected me with the Hakalah program. The program is funded by the Claims Conference, which is funded by settlements with Swiss banks, German corporations, and other guilty parties. It's supposed to pay for "clinical assessments, emergency assistance, home care, assistance with compensation, and restitution claims, advocacy, case management, and free dental care for Nazi victims."

As soon as I started telling the social worker our problems, I knew I'd found a savior. Her name is Ellen, and I could tell she was listening and taking notes. She said all the right things about getting you the care you needed. She cooed and clucked at the right moments in the story. She told me she'd speak to your doctors and talk to lawyers about my power-of-attorney rights. She made me feel like I had an ally, a friend even. We made an appointment for her to meet you. I believed, with chorus-girl optimism, that she'd see how bad you were doing and take the steps to make you better. Ellen would fix everything.

I told you a lady was coming to help us.

"Vhat lady?"

"She's a friend of mine," I stretched, "but this is her job."

"Oh, okay, a friend."

"So make sure you're wearing clothes."

On the day of the appointment you were back in the hospital, so I canceled. But before we could reschedule, Ellen my savior called to tell me that helping you was "beyond the parameters of my job." She passed us along to a caseworker from a different department.

That lady was nice enough, and I'm certain she was trying her best. But her best included ignorance of the system and fear of upsetting people she should have been pressuring for results. She was also pretty good at insults. She once accused me of trying to warehouse you to ease my burden. Maybe that was because she didn't see what I saw. You probably put on the charm when she visited. I wouldn't be surprised if you hit on her.

That was the problem with trying to fix you: You weren't always broken. Once you convinced the supermarket to resurrect their delivery service just for you. When I called that night to nag you about getting out to socialize, you answered the phone from your kitchen.

"Visit people? I got chicken on! I'm a busy man."

The next morning you were hooked up to an EKG again.

One day you took a walk and ate a hamburger. The day after that, you were back on your couch in your underwear, your jaw covered with whiskers, your stomach filled with pills, your suicide plans formulating.

SINATRA

In the wee small hours of the morning, I try to imagine myself in those camps. I lie in my soft warm bed and pretend it's hard and cold. That I'm starving and terrified. Someone could kill me tomorrow, or the next day. Something hurts, beyond the hunger. Many parts of me have been wounded and some haven't healed properly. How could they without food or rest? Now, I tell myself, try to make it.

I never could.

I don't even ski because I get too cold. I can't imagine skipping the cold cereal I eat for breakfast every morning, never mind the nutritious meals. I'm as soft as soft can be.

I play this game when I'm showering, too. What if I couldn't shower for years? Or the only showers were cold trickles of water without soap? When I forget to replace my dirty bath towel and have to pat myself dry with a small hand towel instead, I stop my internal whining by imagining having no towel and having to run wet from shower to bunk during the winter. I play the game when I'm walking outside during the winter. Pretend you're barefoot, I challenge myself. Pretend you have no coat. Try to make it.

Never.

I even think about it when I'm cleaning my house. I ask myself how little I could live with. If someone came and took all of my stuff, what would I really miss? I might not survive any of the physical deprivation that you did, but I'm pretty sure I could walk away from the stuff. Especially if I could take a bag, like your mother did when she left home for the ghetto. This leads to another version of the game: What to take? One pot, one towel, and some soap. Medicine for my kids; at least antibiotic ointment. A book or a journal? A pen or a pencil? A thick blanket, or a thin one with a pillow? What outfit would keep me warmest in the winter but be bearable in the summer? Should I bother packing makeup?

All this is my way of mentally preparing for it to happen again. A lot of Jews must test themselves like this. It's not that hard to imagine being where you were. Take away the ocean and a fistful of decades and we're right there in the cattle cars. And while I don't think it will ever happen again to the Jews, mainly because we're sitting on our rockers with rifles across our collective laps, just in case, it's good to be ready for the worst.

At least while the whole wide world is fast asleep.

APRIL 11, 2010—TWENTY-THREE YEARS PAST PRIMO LEVI

Primo Levi might have fallen.

That's what some people believe. He tumbled over a third-floor railing in his apartment building by accident, they argue, citing evidence such as his good moments prior to dying, and how easy it would have been for him to lose his balance.

Others point out that he was depressed and had written about never shedding his Holocaust demons. It must have been suicide, they say.

I suspect the second group is right. It definitely spoils the survivor fairy tale, though.

Levi was an Italian Jewish chemist who landed in Auschwitz after voluntarily joining a partisan group to fight the bad guys. He survived Auschwitz and went on to write world-famous books about his ordeal. He reunited with his mother after the war, got married, and had kids. His writings seemed optimistic. People were shocked when he died because he'd seemed to have been a champion at surviving. *Why now?* they asked.

Watching you go through old age gave me a hypothesis. Levi was sixty-seven. He'd recently had minor surgery. Maybe he wasn't feeling well. Maybe he decided he had earned the right to never again feel sick, to never again be so out of control of his own body. So he decided to control the outcome himself.

Or perhaps he prayed for an accident, as I sometimes request action that will stop your body from imprisoning you. *Enough,* I sometimes say to God. *Make him feel perfect or let him go.* Maybe that's the conversation Primo had, too.

No one will ever know why Levi's story ended. But you're even older, more physically damaged. Why shouldn't I believe it's possible for you to take the same way out? Even the research backs me up.

A group of Israeli researchers recently looked at the suicide rates of elderly patients in a psychiatric hospital and found that Holocaust survivors had attempted suicide far more often than the other people—24 percent compared to 8 percent.

"The rate of the risk of attempted suicide among Holocaust sur-vivors was significantly increased," the researchers reported. "Aging of survivors is frequently associated with depression, reactivation of traumatic syndromes, physical disorders, loss, and psychological distress, possibly increasing the risk of suicide . . . The growth of the elderly population, of whom many had had traumatic life experiences, emphasizes the need to implement preventive strategies so that sui-cidal risk may be contained."[5]

Remember when you told me that someday you were going to knock on a neighbor's door, hand him a card with my phone number on it, then go home and overdose?

"I won't take the pills today," you said, "but I'm not going to tell you when."

Shit.

"What about me?" I asked. "If you did that, think of how I'd feel knowing I couldn't help you?"

I wanted to tell you that you'd be passing me your despair like you passed me your brown paper bag of memories, but that sounded too dramatic. I wanted to remind you of every time you'd called me your best friend. I wanted to beg you to wait until the doctor found the right combination of drugs. Instead, we just yelled over each other.

I didn't want to commit you, but isn't that what you're supposed to do when someone outlines their plan? I knew inpatient treatment may have helped again, but I couldn't imprison you against your will. I wasn't equipped to make such a decision. We both needed a psychiatrist.

"I'm eighty-eight years old! I don't need no shrink!"

"What are you afraid of?"

"I'm not afraid."

"Yes you are."

"Okay, you want to come get me and bring me, I'll go," you said.

---

5 *American Journal of Geriatric Psychiatry,* August 2005, 13(8):701–4. Increased risk of attempted suicide among aging Holocaust survivors. Barak, Y.; Aizenberg, D.; Szor, H.; Swartz, M.; Maor, R.; Knobler, H. Y. Abarbanel Mental Health Center, 15 KKL Street, Bat-Yam, 59100, Israel.

What? Again with the sudden capitulation? That game was really starting to annoy me.

I made you promise not to kill yourself before I could schedule the appointment.

"Okay, darling. Good-bye."

Then I sat on my front steps and cried.

LUCK

"Tell me again why you think you lived?" I asked.

"Luck," you said.

This is the fourth theory of your survival.

As the Americans approached, thousands of prisoners in the cluster of Dachau camps waited for rescue. The guards surrounding the camps gripped their guns and waited for orders. The whole Nazi operation had been frantically destroying witnesses. They'd marched the healthier inmates away from Dachau. They'd shot people who stumbled. But they still hadn't murdered those of you they'd deemed unworthy of a death march—those they assumed would die on their own. But you held out until the great day that the candy-bearing soldiers arrived. Luck?

"If it was another day before the Americans came, they might have killed everybody."

Luck.

PREMATURE INHERITANCE

Back when you were well, you'd forced a $4,000 check on me.

"I want you to have it before I die," you said.

I didn't want it, but I could tell you felt good being able to give it, so I took the check and put it in the bank. I had no intention of spending it until you actually died. You gave the same amount to Vera's daughter, plus a bigger check to help her pay for Vera's round-the-clock care.

The money came from your reparations. Though the payments resulted from the incident that had taken away all your pride and power, they ironically became the only source of your pride and power: the power to be generous; the pride of being able to care for someone less fortunate.

The reparations are ironic for another reason, too. The purpose of the payments is to make people's lives easier, not to further punish them. It didn't work that way for you.

Later, your giving spirit would bite both of us in the ass.

I told you I didn't want that check.

FALL 2007

The shrink that was covered by your insurance practiced in a big HMO building. I wanted to take you to an expert in old people or Holocaust survivors, but your doctor wouldn't approve any referrals out of his system.

We waited in a long, narrow room with several people in their fifties and a kid with his mother. Nobody spoke or looked at each other, not even the two of us. We were all playing Let's Pretend We're Strangers and No One Will Notice that We're in a Shrink's Office. At 4:30, movement and speech ensued. A teenage girl with swollen red eyes popped out of one room and headed straight for the door as the mother and kid hurried to keep up with her. I felt bad that no one offered her the time or space to get her normal face back. Teenagers hate it when they look as if they've been crying. People usually stare. Her mother would look at her with that annoying concerned expression. Her brother would stay a little too quiet in the backseat, waiting for her to burst again. They should really have a face-clearing room for the teenagers after therapy.

A man wearing a tie and giant eyeglasses appeared in a back doorway. Three of the women and one older man stood up and followed him through the door. I was impressed with their mastery of the stranger game, considering they'd spend the next hour sharing secrets and crying to each other in group therapy.

A young black woman opened another door and called your name. We followed her in.

"I'm Doctor H.," she said.

Oh, boy. This was going to be fun. Young, ethnic, woman—exactly the opposite of the old white doctors you usually trusted.

"Be nice," I whispered firmly into your collar.

Her office was tiny and generic: standard-issue particleboard desk, two cheap metal chairs, a framed poster of a leafless tree in the snow. *Solitude,* it said on the bottom, but it should have said *Despair* for the feeling it imparted. I'd finally gotten you into a shrink's office and she couldn't even choose soothing art.

She asked about your physical symptoms. You handed her a purple gift bag that you'd filled with your pill bottles. She pulled each out and put them into categories: heart, stomach, brain. She tried to talk to you, and even offered a smart assessment. Recent losses, like Vera's departure, might be waking up old losses, like everyone's departure. But you didn't want to talk about that.

At the end of the session, she told you to stop drinking caffeinated tea and to double your anxiety pills. Neither strategy helped at all.

The other doctor was better. David found her, the wife of one of his colleagues. She specialized in geriatrics and happened to be the daughter of Holocaust survivors. She agreed to see you for free.

You were in bad shape that day. You felt carsick from the drive into Boston. You refused lunch, leaned against the hallway wall for support as we entered the building, and insisted on waiting in the lobby while I got some coffee. When I returned, you seemed to be in the throes of a major panic attack, full sweat, budding tears, and all. I calmed you down in her waiting room. The furnishings were plain and old; I couldn't decide if this was intentional, to remind the patients of doctors' appointments when they were in their prime, or an indication of the value they placed on old patients: Give 'em the junk furniture; what do we care?

After asking questions about your drugs, the doctor told you to remember the following three words:

Hair.

Glasses.

Sweater.

Then she asked you to draw a clock with all the numbers on it.

"I never learned to draw," you said in a child's tone.

Your circles were ovals and your first three clocks were too small for us to read, and warped like Picasso's, but you finally got it right.

"Perfect!" the doctor said.

By this time, you'd transformed from basket case to Mr. Perky Flirt, smiling and laughing as she read your medical records. She explained that some of your problems might have been the result of tiny strokes that caused brain changes, which she'd seen manifest in health obsessions before. It could get worse, she said, but it could also get better if you took baby aspirin and walks. Senior activities and socializing wouldn't hurt, either.

"This isn't the only thing that can help you," she said, holding up the list of medicines you were on.

You agreed to get out more. You even nodded when she told you to try harder for me.

Then she returned to the memory test.

"Can you repeat the words I told you at the beginning of our session?"

"Hay-er," you said, and I remembered how charming your Yiddish accent sounds to strangers.

Long pause. You tried to remember. *I* tried to remember.

"The glesses."

You pointed to yours. Another pause.

"The sveh-ter."

The doctor turned to me.

"He doesn't have Alzheimer's."

"No," you said. "I got Youngsheimer's."

And didn't that doctor, just like every other woman you've charmed, just crack up?

It was a great appointment: supportive, encouraging, kind. Also, useless. The next morning I called to check up on you.

"Zoo," you said. "I feel very sick. My right side."

January 9, 2011—Papers, Please

I keep expecting you to abruptly sit up and ask: "You got my papers?"

You arranged and paid for your funeral and gravestone before Bibi died. You've given me multiple copies of the prearrangement contract, canceled checks to the funeral home and the monument company, and the sketches that show the wording you want on your marker. But you are terrified that I'll either lose them or forget to remind the medical authorities.

"In case anything happens—I don't want you to throw me on the side of the road," you said.

It's such a preposterous idea that it sounded like a joke when you first said it. But that night I woke up in the middle of the night and I remembered that that's exactly what happened to so many people during the Holocaust—their dead bodies were tossed onto the road, left to decay without anything close to a proper Jewish burial. Then I realized what all of the calls to 911 had really been about.

"I thought I was gonna die," you'd said.

But the dying wasn't the worst fear, was it? It was the dying alone. It was the side of the road.

I've got your papers. I hope I won't need them yet, but I've got them.

October–November 2007

You brought up the nursing home first.

"Remember we go there a few weeks ago?"

"You mean a few years ago?"

"Years ago?"

"Yeah."

"I felt better after that. Maybe I feel better now."

You wanted to know if you'd be allowed to bring all of your clothes, "or just a couple pair pants."

All of them, I told you.

"I'll come see you every week if you go, you know," I said. "You're not gonna lose me."

"A suit, too?"

"You can bring your suit."

"The rest I put in your basement."

"Anything you want."

"They give you pillows there?"

They give you pillows there? Were you asking if the nursing home is anything like Auschwitz? If you would have to use your shoes as a pillow, the benefit being that they wouldn't get stolen by other inmates?

"Of course they give you pillows," I said. "It's not like the camps, you know."

You smiled, as if to convince both of us that of course you knew that.

I dug out the welcoming letter the social worker had written after our first nursing home visit all those years earlier. I'll just call her up, I thought, tell her what's happening and ask her to book you a room.

But she didn't work there anymore, so I was told to fill out an application instead. I sent it back with a cover letter explaining your special circumstances: *poor, single, childless survivor seeks soothing end-of-life care.* They responded by requiring more paperwork and passing me off to an intern who tried to set my expectations straight when she told me there were lots of other poor Holocaust survivors who'd managed to navigate the system without skipping the line, so, no, they wouldn't be giving you extra help. I found this hard to believe. First of all, how many survivors are left in our area? And of those, how many had no children? And of those, how many worked minimum-wage jobs and lived in subsidized housing? I hardly think "lots" was the accurate word.

But policy is policy and bureaucracy is never-changing. Does it surprise you to hear that the intern gave me the wrong information about the required paperwork, costing us another couple of weeks in frustrating phone calls? Or that the kindness of the first social worker had been expunged from your record? It didn't matter what had happened then; we had to start over. As you entered and exited the ER a few more times, I arranged another tour. On a Friday in November, we were scheduled to take the first step in the process for a second time.

That morning, you called me to cancel. You'd gone a little crazy with the prune juice, spent most of the night on the toilet, and now were too tired. And hopeless.

"How can they help me?" you asked.

"Just let them try!"

I was losing patience with you. I knew you couldn't help it, but your lack of gumption was grinding me down. I informed you that we were going and you'd better be in the lobby when I drove up to your building.

The social worker at the nursing home shook my hand as if she didn't want to touch it. I can't tell you her name, but I can tell you it was ironic. Think: a killer named Angel. Think an obese man named Slim. That's the idea. She had the skin of someone in her fifties and wore a mini skirt. She was very kind to you.

Before you could view the home's finery, she said, the people in the finance office wanted to speak to you. They knew from the forms I'd filled out that you had a few thousand dollars in your bank account, most of it from reparations. I told the finance lady that you'd given away some money, including my $4,000 inheritance, which I would gladly return, plus an unknown amount for Vera's care. She hinted that those gifts might cause a problem with getting Medicaid to pay for your nursing home care, but she wouldn't know how much of a problem until I brought in five years of your bank statements and got rid of some of your savings. Open a burial account, she said. Pad his prepaid funeral package with extras. Medicaid couldn't hold that against you.

The social worker rolled in a wheelchair for your touring pleasure. She showed us all the places we'd seen before. But while we were waiting for an elevator, you saw what you really needed in the next chair: Vera.

Big smiles bloomed on your scared, depressed faces. Later, we went to her room on the all-Russian floor. She couldn't speak to or understand you. It had been a long time since you'd shared a meal, a house key, a bed. Now you sat in separate wheelchairs a yard away from each other. But you bridged all those gaps by reaching your hand toward hers. She reached back and you both leaned forward enough to squeeze each other's fingers. Before we left, you stroked her soft white hair with your big hand.

That was the first good moment of the day. The second came when the social worker informed us that if you needed a short-term interim bed, they could take you immediately. Either way, you would go on the waiting list for a permanent bed if you wanted.

"Would you like to come here?" she asked, leaning down to your level.

"Yeah," you said.

The third good moment happened in the nursing home cafeteria. You ate: two pieces of challah, some lettuce and hard-boiled eggs, a bowl of matzo-ball soup, and a glass of milk. And didn't I kvell, just like all Jewish mothers do.

I wanted to tell the Lady at the Party about our success. Remember her? She was the one who seemed to have my back, to believe, as I did, that you deserved special treatment. She'd called any hassles directed your way a *shanda*—a shame. I'd reached out to her when I was struggling to find agencies to help you stay in your apartment. She didn't actually help, but she was supportive. Her e-mails contained lines like these: "I am sorry to hear the situation is so bad . . . Aron is lucky he has you. So is our community."

I hadn't really needed more than that until the nursing home paperwork hassles began. When I'd let her know how disappointed I'd been in the response to my letter, she'd put in a call to some Head Honchos. Who knows what these people of power say to each other, but I assumed she asked them, Mob style, to "take care of me."

They responded with stories that made me look crazy. They had no knowledge of any letter requesting special consideration. As far as they knew, I'd appeared out of nowhere with you and started making demands. In any case, she reported, they'd offered the interim bed, so everything should be settled.

I figured the social worker was behind my newly earned bad reputation. Making me look bad would distract her superiors from noticing that she'd ignored my "help a survivor" plea. When the Honchos entered the picture, she scolded me for involving them. I ended up apologizing to her. Anything to get you back to the place where so many good things had just happened.

On Monday, they took all those lovely moments, scrunched them into a ball like a bad draft of a poem, and threw them into the trash. There would be no bed for you, emergency or otherwise, until you could pay.

FORGETTING

Living through the Holocaust, you once told me, was like the pain of having a baby.

"This you don't forget," you said.

Ah, but you were wrong. Women *do* forget the pain of childbirth because it ends in joy. Your pain didn't end. It has affected every minute of your life.

"You can't stop thinking about it," you said. "When you're just plain nobody and an evil person comes and takes everything away from you."

You looked at me and went on.

"Your dignity."

NOVEMBER 2007—HEROES OR VILLAINS

It was all a matter of math. It cost $256 a day for the nursing home to house and feed you. You'd never had that kind of money, so you needed to apply for Medicaid. The thing with Medicaid is, they hate it when people give away money. It makes them suspect that the gift was a strategy to make the giver appear poor and therefore qualify for government aid. The biggest worry is that old people will transfer their money and homes to their kids as soon as they realize they need nursing home care. To prevent such fraud, Medicaid examines all large gifts the applicant has made during the previous five years. Whatever they find can count against qualification. It's called a denial period: the number of days it takes to make up what you gave away.

You, of course, had given away almost all of your money, which the nursing home people knew would keep Medicaid from covering you for thirty-nine days. When I explained that the money had been payback for your Holocaust years and couldn't be counted, they corrected me. It couldn't be counted *if* you'd kept it in a separate account instead of depositing it in the same account as your social security checks. But you didn't know that. Even your brother, with his life of conventional success and his accomplished progeny, didn't know that. He'd never kept a separate account, either.

There were options, of course. Apply to Medicaid, then appeal the denial-period decision. Oh, sure, that'd be simple. My unborn grandchildren would probably be dead by the time the issue was resolved, never mind you.

Or, the nursing home people said, you could dig up nearly $10,000 to pay for the thirty-nine days on your own.

"This is the rule," the social worker told me. "This is the way it works. We don't give free care."

That can't be true, I thought. What about the *shanda?* What about all those Jewish advocacy groups?

I asked if the nursing home had a scholarship to cover your denial period. They didn't answer, though one of the Honchos led me to believe it was possible when he wrote: "Our ultimate goal is to help Mr. Lieb, but [we] cannot be expected to be the only party providing the resources to enable his admission to be covered from day one."

The *only* party. That means they'd be *one* of the parties, right?

I asked friends and acquaintances who volunteered for the largest Jewish fund-raising organization if they could connect me with whomever helped Holocaust survivors, but they only pointed me back to the people who had already proved to be useless. I asked Hakalah, the program funded with reparations money, if they could give you a loan. They didn't answer, either, but agreed to negotiate with the nursing home. The social worker told them to stay out of it.

I offered to start raising money, but I couldn't do that until I knew exactly how much you needed. It had taken them a month to figure out your denial period and its cost (something anyone could have calculated after looking at your bank statements for ten minutes), but that still didn't give me a bottom-line figure because no one would tell me what the nursing home would contribute. They just kept telling me to find the money.

The Lady at the Party, who could have probably paid your way with her parking-meter change, must have gotten nervous. She bowed out and told me to deal with the nursing home director instead.

"This is taking place in his institution, and he needs to sort it out," she wrote. "I will stay out of it from here. I hope this sorts itself out."

Sorts *itself* out? What about her? Didn't she lead me to believe she had my back? Hadn't she set me up to expect the Survivors' Special for you? Who should be feeling *shanda* now?

Maybe it got too dirty for her to intervene; people only have so much political capital. Or maybe she believed them when they tried to make me the villain—because now the Honchos were pissed. One accused me of hoarding your money for myself. Another told me to "lower the volume," and called me "judgmental and self-righteous," as if it were an insult.

And you just kept getting worse. The same day they revoked the offer of an emergency bed, you didn't answer my morning phone calls. Two of them. I drove the kids to school, went to the bank to request five years of your statements, then knocked on your door.

"Come in," you croaked.

I had a moment of relief—maybe you'd just been in the shower—until I saw you sitting in your pajamas, your fly open, the *shmatte* on your head. Your voice was ragged as you described your night. You were cold at four in the morning, even after pulling on a second blanket, so you called 911. Our town's ambulance refused to come, so you, ever resourceful, called the fire department in the next town over. They brought you to the ER where they discovered you had low potassium and gave you a prescription for supplements. You cried until I left to fill it.

Two days after that, you called 911 for the last time.

Busy Bees

While all this was happening, everyone was busy. The Honchos were in the middle of working out deals to secure $457 million in loans so they could build a new senior living community. They were writing thank-you notes to private donors to the project, including a couple that tossed in $20 million.

The social service agency charged with helping local Holocaust survivors was making sure it spent its budget—which is funded by Nazi paybacks—fairly.

The Lady at the Party was managing a $40 million family foundation.

Business as usual.

WWEWS? (What Would Elie Wiesel Say?)

Elie Wiesel was probably in town around this time. He teaches at Boston University, so I assume he's close by at least once a week. I never contacted him for help, though I probably could have.

When Carrie was a few days old, I had my second crazy Holocaust experience. Unlike at Dachau, it wasn't a vision. Just a powerful feeling of connection. As I held her and fell deeply in love, I thought about all the young Jewish mothers who had done and felt exactly the same. They'd been where I was, but they'd had their gifts taken away: the love, the pride, the actual babies in some cases. I felt so grateful to be me in my time instead of them in theirs.

I decided—now here's the crazy part—that I wanted to tell someone who'd been there that I wasn't taking my life for granted; that I knew how blessed I was. I couldn't write to those dead mothers, but I could send something to Elie Wiesel.

Carrie had gigantic cheeks, and we had a photo of her at about six months old, smiling the cheekiest smile you can imagine. In that photo, she is the opposite of a hungry, frightened baby living under Nazi rule. She is proof that they failed; that happy, healthy Jewish babies were still abundant in the world.

I mailed the photo to Mr. Wiesel with a note expressing my goofy, embarrassing feelings. He wrote back and thanked me for sending "the smile of your child," and wishing us the best.

I didn't ask him for help with you and our predicament precisely because he had been so kind back then. I couldn't have borne it if he'd disappointed me, too.

November 2007

I had just finished another frustrating meeting with the finance officials, followed by a brief weep in the ladies' room, when the nursing home synagogue caught my eye.

Okay, God, I thought, *it's your turn.*

The synagogue door was closed, but that didn't mean the room was empty. Sometimes the otherworldly hide in the most obvious places.

I pulled open the door, hoping to find God lounging about so I could ask her to fix everything.

An old man wrapped in a *tallit* sat in one of the seats near the front. He was either sleeping or praying, but he was certainly alone. Not a whiff of God.

I considered sitting far away from him and waiting. Maybe God would show up and plant a solution in my head. Maybe God would explain why I had anything to do with this mess. Maybe something would burst into flames.

Maybe I'm an idiot, I thought.

I was starting to doubt that there was any bigger meaning, other than the obvious: People can be assholes. You hadn't been put in my path to teach me something; there was no lesson here. No heartwarming ending that would put all your suffering in perspective. It doesn't always work that way. There hadn't been a meaningful ending for your little sisters, had there?

The synagogue looked so peaceful and it had been such a bad day already. But I wasn't sure about the rules. Maybe I wasn't allowed in there. The people who ran the place already thought I was a threat. With my luck, they'd accuse me of trespassing, kick me out, and ban me from the building forever. Then how could I help you?

I shut the door and walked away. The man hadn't stirred the whole time I'd been peering in.

WHY WE MET

The first time I asked your opinion on why we met, you said it was because I was "there."

I wasn't letting you get away with that.

"Why did you talk to Max and me that day?"

"I liked your eyes."

"What about them?"

I was fishing for something about allure and beauty. Instead, you opened your eyes as wide as you could and darted your eyeballs back and forth to demonstrate.

"My eyes were beady? That's what you liked?"

"Not *beady*. They were . . ."

You couldn't find the right word. The Yiddish description must not translate accurately.

"You looked like trouble."

I think the folks who were managing your case would have agreed with you.

THE RIGHTEOUS GENTILES

The kindest people in this part of the story were not Jewish. I hope that's just a coincidence.

After dozens of medical professionals processed you through the same emergency rooms with the same complaint leading to the same frustrating outcome, one finally looked at you from a different angle.

"We're admitting him for 'failure to thrive,'" the nurse named Maryann told me.

Failure to thrive. Just like when you were a newborn and your mother presented you to the rabbi.

That nurse saw that you weren't eating or drinking. She knew that you couldn't take care of yourself anymore and were in danger of dying from something other than chest pains. She knew you couldn't go home again. And she convinced the doctors.

I could have cleaned a week's worth of bedpans for her.

The "custodial care" consisted of a few nights in the hospital followed by an efficient transfer to a temporary nursing home. And who paid for this care? Your regular health insurance on a Medicaid-pending basis, just as it would have if the big nursing home had come through with that interim bed. But why quibble now?

The other Righteous Gentile in our tale was supposed to keep me in line. He was the muscle, the tough guy, The Enforcer. The Honchos had put this man, one of their business office employees, in charge of me.

"You're pushing hard and I won't be pushed," he said, responding to my request for speedier paper-pushing. His voice sounded about one degree removed from rage.

I knew that tone. I come from generations of that tone. I was raised in a house full of that tone.

Now here was someone I could talk to.

After we discussed bank statements and time frames, I tried to get him to see, as most of his colleagues had not, that I wasn't some grifter trying to take advantage of the system. I was just trying to help a guy who had nobody.

"I'm not even related to this man," I said.

"For what it's worth, Sue, uh, Ms. Resnick, I have power of attorney for six people here because nobody else in this building would do it. I have to clean someone's apartment out this weekend. I know what it's like on your end."

Oh, I could *really* talk to this man.

When we met in person, his appearance was as defined as his no-bullshit manner. He wore an elegant gray suit, and his white handlebar mustache was curled at the ends with wax. It didn't seem weird or pretentious, but rather, authentic. Here was a real person with real preferences who was confident enough to show the world his true self—someone with no need to lie.

I'd gone to his office to deliver some document related to your case. We sat at a round conference table, me with a swollen folder of your records and he with a giant stack of forms. He had very blue, very round, very large eyes that looked straight at me. They were eyes that hid nothing, even the truth that I had been trying to dodge with my naiveté and optimism.

"We are not interested in taking Mr. Lieb if Medicaid won't pay for him," he said.

Or maybe he said "if these issues can't be resolved." I was writing down what he said in a reporter's notebook—I wrote down what everyone said—but my hand seemed to freeze on the second part of the statement as I absorbed its clear meaning: no money, no entrance.

No loan, then, right?

The Enforcer didn't know about a loan, a scholarship, or any sort of charity coming out of his organization.

"Would you want the facility to take it on the chin?" he asked incredulously, as if a Jewish nursing home taking a loss to help a Holocaust survivor was the craziest thing he'd ever heard.

You'd think this would have made me really pissed-off at the guy. But it didn't. For once, someone was telling me the truth. I could finally see that the space behind me, where I'd imagined deep-pocketed, grand-hearted people were standing, was vacant.

ORDERS

They were just following orders, right? They had a certain budget and they were going to stick with it. They had printed Medicaid rules and unspoken inner-circle codes of conduct.

This is the way it works.

Still, it reminded me of them. Following orders is neat. Following consciences can get sloppy. And dangerous. People driven by the need for self-preservation aren't crazy about danger. Guards and neighbors followed orders so they wouldn't get killed. Perhaps nursing home administrators followed orders so they wouldn't get fired.

NOVEMBER 2007

The temporary nursing home that was your way station between your old life and this one wasn't so bad. When I look back on it, maybe we should have stayed there. The people, from the head nurse with her thick Irish brogue to the aide with the voice that reminded me of piña coladas, cared. They tried to make you happy. One day I came in to find you going over the day's menu with a very patient young aide. She'd suggest a food and you'd veto it. *Too greasy* was the usual complaint.

"Eat the minestrone," I interrupted. "It's good for you."

"Be quiet, Gracie," you ordered.

The doctors—when they showed up and remembered to put in prescriptions for the drugs we'd discussed—were compassionate. The one wearing the yarmulke offered to ask his Orthodox community to help you. He didn't understand why the Jewish nursing home wouldn't take you first and then figure out how to afford you.

"Come on," he said. "This is what we're supposed to be doing."

The psychologist they assigned looked like a movie shrink. He wore a slightly tattered tweed blazer, a full beard, and glasses that were a little too something—big? Out of style? I couldn't decide.

You were lying in bed with a rag on your head when he came in. Most of the lights were off and your roommate had ceased blasting Christmas carols for a while. A writer would have described the room as peaceful.

The doctor pressed his palms lightly on your sternum, the place you always point to when trying to describe the pain. He asked you to push against him with your chest.

"Again," he said, as you learned how to take a deep breath.

He asked me if I was a social worker, and when I explained our relationship and the journey we'd been on, he said, "I guess he's just fallen through the cracks."

You continued to calm yourself. Then you spoke.

"In Poland, they used to say, 'You Jews all stick together.' Yeah— the rich with the rich, and the poor with the poor."

The doctor didn't argue.

But even with those good people trying to take care of you, you weren't improving. Despite the numbing patches they stuck to your arms and medicines they handed you in paper cups, you were still in bad shape. Besides your near-constant pain and anxiety, you had a festering foot sore. And you didn't fit with the rest of the patients, a mix of young and old, legless and deranged, mute and hostile. Everyone agreed that the big Jewish nursing home would be the best place for you. I just needed to gather the cash.

MARCH 2010

"Aren't we having a Seder this year?" David asked one Sunday. He'd just returned from a business trip in Israel and was all charged up on primary-source Judaism. Have I mentioned that I've never been to Israel?

"I hate Passover," I announced. "I'm not doing a Seder."

Do you know what's involved in hosting a Seder? Probably not, since you're a man of a certain age. I'll tell you: cooking, cooking, cooking, and more cooking. Have I mentioned that I don't like to cook?

I've been trying to get David to take over the food and nutrition department of our household for a long time. He's much better at it than I am, with his methodical nature, scientific accuracy, and tendency to obsess about details. The way he bounces from one passion to another means it wouldn't be too difficult for him to adjust to being head chef. He could transfer the time he spends bike riding and spreading mulch to planning meals, buying ingredients, and making big leftover-laden meals. He hasn't accepted the offer yet, but my Seder refusal seemed to temporarily inspire him.

"Okay, I'll do it," he said.

I spent the Seder luxuriating like a guest, eating his spectacular brisket, and sipping the lovely kosher wine he'd chosen. I was actually having conversations with relatives instead of waiting on them. It was lovely. Then the phone rang.

A woman said you needed to talk to me. When you got on the phone, you were so upset that I thought someone died. You'd never called me at night before.

"It's so terrible," you said.

"What?"

"She's . . ."

"Who?"

"She, you know, she can't—Bibi. She can't get in here to get me. And I have nobody. I'm all alone here."

Bibi? Dead-eighteen-years Bibi?

I moved to the family room where I could talk to you privately.

"Do you know where you are?"

"Yeah," you said. "The place you see me yesterday. I need you to come."

Now? Honestly, I didn't want to come. On this of all nights, I didn't want to come.

I told you it was raining—you old people seem to hate to make anyone drive in the rain. I told you I had guests over for Passover.

"It's nine in the morning," you said.

"No, it's night. Eight-fifteen."

"Nine?"

"Almost nine. At night."

Then you returned, as though our conversation had shocked you back to the present like a defibrillator to the brain.

"Oh," you said, sounding a little embarrassed. "I didn't know it was night. Okay, I'll talk to you tomorrow."

"Well, I can talk more now," I said. Who cared about the company in the other room?

"No, I'll talk to you tomorrow. You'll come tomorrow?"

Yes. Of course I'd come.

NOVEMBER 2007

"Doesn't he have any family who can help?" one of the honchos asked.

Were these people fucking kidding me? Family? No, he doesn't have any family. Why the hell do you think I'm the one getting kicked around by you assholes?

Okay, you do have family. You have Bill. And that's no small thing. You still talk to each other on the phone almost every week. You still have one blood relative on this Earth. That gives you roots and a connection to who you used to be.

But as far as family you can count on when you're down, they're gone.

The first time I called Bill in New Jersey, back when I was just trying to write about how your life intersected with Vera's, he was suspicious. What did I want from you? he asked. Fair enough. We've all heard stories on the news about home health aides and companions who bilk elderly people out of their fortunes. That you had no fortune made this suspicion a little ridiculous, but I appreciated that he was looking out for you.

The next time I called him, he had softened. I wanted his blessing before signing the papers that would make me your health-care proxy. I figured since he was technically your next of kin, I owed him the chance to take over your care himself. He had no problem letting me do it.

"Sometimes a good friend is more than family," he said. "Family, you have no choice."

He added that if you trusted me, he trusted me.

Still, I dreaded calling him to ask for money. What could be more awkward? But I had to do it. The nursing home certainly wasn't going to help you before I tapped every possible resource. I knew he was comfortable if not wealthy, and that he cared about you. Maybe the difficult conversation would bring all the nonsense to an end.

I called Bill, reminded him who I am, and explained the situation.

"I haven't got money," he said. "I had it, but I lost it in the stock market."

He then proceeded to tell me that you'd created this situation for yourself by giving your money to strangers. He pointed out that you hadn't given any of your money to his kids, though I'm fairly certain they never needed it, and that he was remembering incorrectly. You still have a card from one of them thanking you for the money you sent to his new baby. The note said the gift would go into a college fund.

"What can I do?" he said. "There's got to be some organization that can help him."

Bill has probably only seen the good side of Jewish organizations. The Joint—the American Jewish Joint Distribution Committee—brought him to the United States a year and a half after you arrived. Perhaps he stayed in Germany longer because he grew comfortable living with his German girlfriend and her family. You were the one who told him not to bring her to the States. His wife of fifty-something years should appreciate you for that.

He met his wife in New York while he was working in a manufacturing business. After a few years of learning to make car seating and convertible tops, he and a few partners opened their own shop in New Jersey. When the partnership dissolved, he started a new company by himself. He went on to live the classic American up-by-your-bootstraps story. He and his wife bought a nice house, had two sons, dressed them in tuxedos that matched his at least two times, according to the posed photos, for who knows what events (bar mitzvahs? cruises? fancy-dress balls for upholsterers?), and educated them well. They gave Bill five grandchildren to spoil.

The awkwardness of our phone conversation wasn't over. I knew the nursing home would want me to dig as deep as possible. What about his sons, the medical men? Bill had sent you pictures of their black-tie weddings and bar mitzvahs. One of them had mailed out printed, embossed Jewish New Year cards.

"Do you think your sons could help?" I asked.

He didn't like that question. He was adamant: He would never ask his sons to help you because you were "never good to them."

"You know how he is," Bill said.

"I think he's very nice and warm," I answered. Brother or not, no one bad-mouths you in my presence without a rebuttal.

He claimed that you were always kinder to friends than to family. He cited as an example a time when you stashed chocolate away rather than sharing it when you were a kid in Zychlin.

Who can ever know what really goes on between family members? All I have is the knowledge that you and Bill's wife despise each other, and the fact that you still have pictures of his children and grandchildren all over your room. I don't know the whys behind either of those circumstances. I just know that after talking to your brother, I felt more alone than ever.

JANUARY 9, 2011

Fuck you.

That's the one Yiddish swear you wouldn't teach me, claiming there's no translation for it. But I looked it up.

Gai tren zich.

Don't worry. Even if I said it to all the people who deserved to hear it, the way I screw up languages, they'd never know what I was talking about.

If this is it, if you really don't wake up, I'll never hear your catch-phrases again. Oh how I love the way you use language.

The day I asked if you wanted to come to High Holiday services with me: "I'd be like a dead pigeon before I go there."

The day you tried to apologize for involving me: "When I'm gone with the wind it will be a lot less trouble for you."

The day you wanted to express your extreme displeasure with greasy scrambled eggs: "I eat that, I be sick like a cat."

Whenever you were making a serious point: "Listen good."

All the days you wanted to know about me: "What's news with you?"

What's news with me?

My best friend appears to be dying.

CHEESE/MENSCH

The Big Cheese of Boston Holocaust survivors, the main specimen at ceremonies and anniversaries, the spokesman for all of you, told me the truth.

"There is no safety net," he said in an accent like yours, although with a bit more polish to it. "There is money for Holocaust causes, but it goes in the wrong direction."

One of the social workers admitted the same thing. She said donors give to Holocaust museums and memorials, and to schools and social groups charged with preserving the Jewish community, but there's no fund specifically earmarked for survivors. Even the Claims Conference money allotted to agencies like hers isn't exclusively for people like you. It's also shared with impoverished Soviet refugees who may or may not have experienced direct Holocaust horrors.

"The needs of actual survivors aren't being met," she said.

Why don't we weave a safety net? We'll use the reparations money you've saved in the last few months to form a nonprofit that will help anyone else who had a bad life and deserves a good death. We can even call it that: The Good Death Fund. But there would be rules. Not just any bad life would count; this fund would be for genocide survivors only. Nationality or religion wouldn't matter; we'll take applications from Armenians, Cambodians, Tutsi—anyone who's outlived their enemy's final solution.

When things get bad for them, they won't have to wait for help. We'll never accuse them of threatening suicide as a cry for attention, as one of the Honchos did. At the end of their lives, they'd get a break.

It would be like the tiny group of people who manage a modest fund billed as Boston's Jewish Safety Net. When I told the guy in charge of it about you, he offered to give you an interest-free loan. We were working out the details when strangers came to the rescue, but I will always be grateful to him. His kindness was such a welcome tonic after speaking to another so-called good guy who got my hopes up.

The Big Cheese, after hearing the resources I'd exhausted, told me to call a man who gave a lot of money to Holocaust causes and social service agencies.

I was skeptical.

"What's his interest in this?" I asked.

"He's a good Jew," The Big Cheese said. "He's a mensch."

I called this mensch immediately.

He said he couldn't talk for long because he worked at home as a stockbroker and was very busy. But he took enough time to listen to the abridged version of your saga and offered to set up a conference call with the bloodless stones we'd already tried to tap. He couldn't figure out why The Big Cheese had recommended him. He wasn't a social worker, he informed me, and only gave money to a Holocaust cause once.

"I'm not sure why he told me to call you either," I said. "He said you were a good Jew and a mensch, and I was looking for one of those."

"I hope I am," he said. "But I can't just hand out money to people."

I didn't bother to tell The Big Cheese.

JANUARY 9, 2011

The next time we speak, I'm going to insist that you tell me the secret. You know the one—about your wife. The terrible thing she did during your marriage? The thing your brother hinted about but said you'd have to tell me? When I asked, you refused.

"No," you said. "I tell you about the war, yes. But not that. It's private."

Private? More private than insinuating that she went down on you before you were married?

I let it go, but every once in a while I'd ask again.

"So, what was that thing your wife did?"

"Ah," you'd say with the hand wave. "Never mind!"

"I promise I won't write about it. Come on. Just tell me."

"No," you'd say, and I could tell you weren't going to budge. I think your stubbornness is really the secret to your survival. Hitler said die and you said no. End of story.

It's been a while since I asked about the secret. Come on. Wake up and gimme a little gossip.

DECEMBER 2007

It was time to beg. I spent two days composing a fund-raising letter explaining your situation and sent it to every Jew in my e-mail address file. I told them about our stupid predicament, why you needed help from outside the system, and what I'd done already. I even managed to tattle.

"Some big players in the Jewish philanthropic community are aware of the situation, but they have declined to help."

God, I wish I could have named names.

Within a half-hour of pressing SEND, the principal of the kids' religious school called.

"I worked at Yad Vashem in Israel," he said. "I know all about this problem."

Even in Israel, Holocaust survivors aren't necessarily revered. The *Jerusalem Post* reported that 33 percent of them are in need. Other reports put the number higher.

Perhaps the Israelis would like to borrow my letter. It actually yielded results. Family members offered cash. Kids turned over their leaf-raking money. Two guys who had sons on Max's Little League teams and mothers who'd survived the Holocaust sent me checks. The wife of one of the guys told me they felt better giving their money to an actual person rather than to a charity. They were happy to be involved, she said, and other people would be, too.

"You've got people behind you now, she said."

Well, what do you know? Humanity was back in the building. I still couldn't pay for those denied days, but it was an encouraging start.

A few people shared connections.

One friend put me in touch with a Medicaid lawyer, who agreed to on-the-house assistance if I wanted to bring a hardship case against Medicaid. I appreciated the offer but declined his help. I didn't have the energy to take on a government agency, and frankly, my beef wasn't with Medicaid. I understood the rationale behind their policies. Besides, they aren't my people. They weren't breaking my heart.

An acquaintance wrote and said he had "pushed buttons" at the nursing home. He knew a nurse who worked there, and "could get anything done."

"I am told that Aron should be getting in immediately," he claimed.

A couple of people scolded me, gently, for expecting too much of Jewish organizations. Remember, they said, such charities are pulled in many directions. They're overwhelmed with demands to fund institutions that strengthen the Jewish community, such as Jewish schools.

"Yeah, yeah," I said, because I didn't want to be rude.

But honestly, I didn't understand that argument. Aren't we trying to build and strengthen the community in large part *because* the Holocaust knocked it down? So isn't neglecting the Holocaust victims the ultimate hypocrisy?

1940–1941

The Germans didn't believe you had worked in the Zychlin ghetto because, get this—you didn't have proof. I guess you left your pay stubs in your file cabinet in Dachau, along with all the other records you'd toted through the necropolis Europe had become.

I found the rejection letter in your dresser drawer when I was searching for some bank statement or another.

"Your claim for Social Security (Ghetto-Work) is NEGATIVE."

Germany's social security is similar to ours. In both countries, people contribute a percentage of their earnings while working, then collect during retirement. Apparently, there had been a chance for survivors to apply for the pensions even though they'd neglected to have the money taken out of their checks during the war.

Later we'd fill out the forms again. The law had changed. It turns out you could qualify for the retirement pension if you could prove that you'd worked willingly in the ghetto. You had to show that you voluntarily smashed stones on streets behind the Zychlin police station while being watched by people with sticks and guns, as opposed to being forced to do it.

"Nobody volunteered," you said as we filled out the forms together. "There was no work."

I was pissed that we had to deal with the stupid paperwork, but you insisted. I wrote while you threw out one-liners.

"Wit' my luck, I get laid off from the ghetto!"

I included a note about the German government's cruelty in getting your hopes up when they'd already rejected you. I doubted that you would receive anything more than another rejection, but I dutifully mailed the forms to Mrs. Glucksburg, a lady in Florida. I'm still not sure why she's involved, though I think she's the go-between for the survivors and the German lawyers.

About a year later, my cell phone rang.

"This is Mrs. Glucksburg," a German-accented voice said.

Who?

"A large amount of money is coming from Germany," she said.

Oh, *that* Mrs. Glucksburg. The ghetto reparations lady.

"Oh, hi," I said.

"Yes, hello. How is your father?"

"He's fine," I said. "He's not my father."

She rolled on with her speech. She wanted the mailing address. She told me you would be getting a small monthly payment for the rest of your life, along with a lump sum to make up for the money you should have been getting since your first application.

Crap, I thought. More money to deal with.

"Will the checks be made out to him or to me?"

"No, checks cannot be made out to anyone but him," she says. "And when he dies you will tell us."

"So since I have power of attorney . . ."

She didn't let me finish. The conversation was over.

"The check will be mailed to you. Good-bye."

Then she hung up.

I guess it was good news for you to get the same social security as all of Germany's old folks, but not for me. I'd have to open another account so these funds wouldn't mix with the checking account I used to pay your phone bill and jeopardize your Medicaid eligibility. I'd have to bring you a second check to sign every month. I'd have to worry that you'd notice that one check was made out to me and one made out to you, something I'd successfully hidden until then so you wouldn't freak out.

The pension didn't arrive for so long that I figured Mrs. Glucksburg had spent it. When it finally came, it was years too late to be of any help.

DECEMBER 2007—THE IDEA

My sister-in-law came up with the idea: Why didn't we loan you the money and repay ourselves with the reparations checks that would keep coming in as long as you lived?

Wait, we could do that? Wouldn't Medicaid have some objection?

Nope, The Enforcer told me, it wouldn't be a problem as long as we could show that the money was in an account under your name. They didn't care where it came from. He even typed up a promissory note for all of us to sign to make the arrangement legal. According to the nursing home social worker, with the loan in the works, you could get a bed as soon as one became available. They trusted me to come through with the payment.

All of which begged this question: Why the hell hadn't any of the officials thought of this solution as soon as they knew they wouldn't be pitching in? They're the ones who were supposed to know the system.

I had no idea we could play with your reparations money that way, but shouldn't they have known? A loan: how obvious.

But before we could decide which kid's college account to plunder, and before I could write a letter telling my friends I didn't need their help anymore, the Hanukkah miracle occurred.

A Brief Recounting of the Hanukkah Story

Pretend for a moment that Hanukkah isn't really a minor holiday pumped up to give Jewish kids a chance for merriment and gift-opening during the Christmas month. Focus instead on the miracle.

The Syrians were the newest Jew haters in town. While trying to stop us from practicing Judaism and otherwise do away with us, they trashed the big temple in Jerusalem. The Jewish bad-boy Maccabees defeated the Syrians, then got everyone to help fix up the temple for rededication. There was a lighting problem. They could only find enough olive oil to burn the eternal lamp, which illuminates the Torah, for one day.

According to the version I learned in Sunday school, they sent someone to get more oil, an errand that would take eight days. Surely, the light would be out by the time he returned. But wonder of wonder, miracle of miracles, it kept burning the whole eight days.

Some people criticize the elaborateness of Hanukkah because they say it celebrates a military victory.

Some people got no respect for miracles.

December 11, 2007—The Righteous Jews

> *A Jew must believe in miracles. If a Jew don't believe in miracles, he is not a realist.*
> —Simon Wiesenthal, Nazi hunter

I had e-mailed my fund-raising letter to the rabbi of the temple I belonged to (but barely attended). He said he couldn't forward my entire letter to the congregation, but he could send out a condensed version. He ended his appeal to them like this: "You will not get a tax deduction or any other reward for your generosity—only the satisfaction of doing what is good in the eyes of God."

That hit a nerve. People didn't press DELETE. They must have run to their checkbooks, because only a few days later, on the last day of Hanukkah, I pulled a four-inch stack of envelopes out of my mailbox. All of them contained something for you.

I read the amounts as Carrie wrote them down. The checks ranged from $15 to $500, but added up to thousands. I recognized almost none of the donors. Some attached notes thanking us, blessing us, throwing the word *mitzvah* around. Some wrote to you:

"I know what it is to have no family, as I also came from the immagration [sic]."

"May life be good to you."

But most of them hadn't bothered with a note. They just wrote checks and stuck them in business envelopes. Added to the money already donated, we actually had enough. Soon we had too much. As donations continued to arrive throughout the month—$5 in one envelope, a second payment from someone who thought she hadn't given enough—I had to call people to ask whether they wanted me to destroy their checks or send them back. In total, more than eighty-five people gave money to help you. You were right—the (relatively) poor Jews do stick together.

I called The Enforcer with the news.

He told the social worker that we officially had enough money to cover your denial period. Then the strangest thing happened: They found a bed for you. Two hours after calling The Enforcer, I received this e-mail from the social worker:

Sue: Congratulations on your hard work. I know this has been a long, hard road for both of you. As it happens, there is an appropriate male bed which opened yesterday. I am pleased to offer it to Aron for Monday, if that works for both of you.

The cynical part of me was sure they'd been denying you entry until the cash arrived. But maybe the filled coffers had nothing to do with the acceptance letter. It could have been that the favor my button-pushing acquaintance requested a week earlier had come through. He called on that same Hanukkah day to ask if I'd heard anything yet. He wasn't surprised when I told him that you'd just been accepted.

"I told you it would be immediately," he said.

His contact insisted on remaining anonymous, so I could never confirm whether she'd had any influence.

But most likely, neither the money nor the favor made the difference. It may have been Fishel Owide, the man you replaced. He'd lived in your room and slept in your bed. He was, like you, a concentration camp survivor who had lost everyone except one brother, and who had a wife but no children. He had worked in Boston's Jewish heartland, too. He was a barber. I bet he cut your hair. I bet you served him a sandwich.

He'd died the previous day at age ninety-six. He must have known you needed a turn.

DECEMBER 17, 2007—MOVING DAY

I had less than a week to get you ready for the rest of your life. Among my chores:

Call phone company to set up nursing home account.

Call phone company to cancel apartment account.

Pay bills: phone, cable, temporary nursing home.

Buy small TV for nursing home room.

Find boxes for packing up cards and photos.

Call nursing home: Who will do his laundry?

Pack all winter clothes, plus sneakers, dress shoes, snow boots, dark suit, and every tie.

Store white shoes and all summer clothes.

Buy storage boxes.

Send Bill new phone number.

Send Germans new address.

Sell car.

Sell furniture.

Cancel car insurance.

Give notice on apartment.

Forward mail.

Write thank-you notes.

Label clothes in permanent ink.

I also had to get you prepared mentally. The good news threw you into a minor tizzy. First you wanted to go to your apartment to supervise the packing. Then you felt too sick. Then you started to obsess about the burial papers again. At least you weren't crying much. The big flood would come a few weeks later, when it hit you that you'd reached your final destination. You missed your old life, your days with Vera, your independence. You wept for an afternoon, then carried on, like a good survivor.

On moving day, I parked in front of the main doors to unpack your belongings. There wasn't much. Everything you needed to live in half a room fit into three plastic boxes and two suitcases. The bigger one was old and had no wheels, so when I carried it down the hall from your apartment, I listed to one side, like the people who carried their lives with them to trains.

Once a staffer helped me pile your stuff onto one of those rolling carts that bellhops use, I got back into my car to move it to the visitor lot. As I turned the key, guess who walked right in front of my car like a black cat? The headest of head Honchos, that's who. I was but one reflex away from giving him judgmental and self-righteous with my gas pedal.

But if I had, I would have missed all the sweetness that was happening inside.

"You're on so many medications!" a doctor said as she examined you. "Is it okay if I get you off some of them?"

"You're the doctor," you said. "You do whatever you want."

That meant you trusted her. You can tell instantly whether people are trustworthy.

She rebandaged your bad foot and ordered a dermatology consult. She made a plan to wean you off your toxic dosages of Extra Strength Tylenol. She took your blood pressure, still your favorite activity.

I was probably beaming. Finally, you were being looked after.

It continued at lunch. The young guy who ran the kitchen went Jewish-mother on you because you didn't like your hamburger and would only eat canned fruit and applesauce.

"He has to eat!" he said.

I wanted to laugh. Compared to the rice and pills repast you'd been eating at home, fruits were fine. But I loved that the cook was worrying about you already.

Everyone we met seemed to know us. We were Bonnie and Clyde. We were Natasha and Boris. Legends.

"Oh, *you're* Sue Resnick," several people said.

Your new social worker seemed afraid of me, as if she'd been warned that I could detonate at any time. She kept saying things like, "We're not perfect, but we do our best," and, "You can call me for anything and I will *always* call you back."

I, in turn, behaved like the most docile and appreciative client she'd ever had, which must have been confusing to her, though quite amusing to me.

I left feeling great. The odyssey was over. You were safe to die in your sleep.

You were free to live happily ever after.

∽

But of course, you didn't.

Part 2:
Being Here

DECEMBER 2007

At first it was great. Two days after arriving, you turned eighty-eight. I gave you a sweater, shirt, and hat from L.L. Bean. You rewarded me with a big hug and multiple kisses on my cheek.

"You say I never kiss you," you said.

I wasn't the only beneficiary of your affection. You called me in a frenzy during that first week.

"Zoo! I need the blue thing in the closet by the door."

Come again?

You'd been hounding me to bring you a suit and razor blades, none of which are blue. But David figured it out—you wanted your blue blazer to wear to dinner. Also, $500 in cash.

Because, by golly, there were chicks here. Granted, most of them wore bibs or didn't have teeth, but you found the hottest chick on the floor. She was only sixty-five and seemed to have all her mental faculties. You were already sitting with her at every meal and hanging out with her in the hallways. Now you wanted to impress her with a bankroll or buy her something from the gift shop, which I don't think sells anything that costs more than $10. I could tell you were in serious crush mode when you dragged me to her room for introductions, then sulked because she'd been yawning as you told our story.

"Don't take it personally," I said. "It was naptime. And you should slow down. Girls don't like when guys come on too strong."

Now I had to be your romantic advisor? I guess it was better than coaxing you away from the pill bottle.

You didn't take my advice, anyway. Instead, you took off your pants in her room.

"He went into her room and, well, he undid his pants and . . . ," the social worker told me.

"*What?*"

"It was fine—these things happen. But she got upset. She just isn't interested in anything like that."

Dude, what were you thinking? After what we went through to get you into this Harvard of nursing homes, you go acting like a state

193

college frat boy? At least the woman forgave you. She continued to be your constant companion for the next two years.

Your penis almost made another appearance in those early days.

"He got angry at someone who was sitting in his chair," the social worker said, "so he started to take off his belt and yell."

Were you fucking kidding me?

I don't know if you were threatening someone with sexual violence or trying to prove your dominance over the seating area by producing your schlong or simply attempting to clear the hallway by standing pantless until you got your chair back. In any case, I repeat: Were you fucking kidding me?

I was terrified that they'd kick you out. The next time I visited, I heard your voice before I could see what you were up to. It was loud. Oh, please don't let him be making trouble, I prayed. Then I saw that you were with a nurse and both of you were cracking up. She told me that you enchanted everyone. I'd hear that a lot: that you could make the emotional shut-ins speak, that you could get tables of silent ladies to laugh. You even looked appealing with your red flannel shirt tucked into khakis, a clean shave, and a smile. You were back.

JANUARY 2008

While you were settling into your new environment, I was shoveling out your old one.

You weren't a hoarder, but there was still a lot of shit to get rid of. I didn't need or want any of it except for your record collection. One of your neighbors came by while I was sorting through your kitchen drawers. The only thing of value, I told her, was your TV. Hey—she needed a TV. I helped her carry it to her apartment.

That was stupid. Without the TV, I had no soundtrack for the undertaking. I continued to go through your stuff in silence. You owned so many clothes. I mean, how many sweater vests could you wear? I understood the healthy collection of winter and summer pajamas because, surprise, I have one, too. But all those sweater vests—I guess that's what happens after you spend years with no clothes of your own.

I found a few other items to distribute: photo albums of Bibi's family, which I eventually sent to her sister; many boxes of Old Spice aftershave, which still sit in your nightstand; a set of china that I gave to a friend. The rest had to go.

I posted an ad:

Apartment Sale
Items include: Twin bed frame and mattresses, dresser and mir-
ror, large, comfortable couch, living-room chair, hope chest /
table, end table with storage, several lamps—some casual, some
may be antiques—hand-tiled coffee table, kitchen table with four
chairs, pots, pans, flatware, dishes, cups, glasses—all kitchen sup-
plies. Also: towels, bed linens, men's clothing, wall mirror, candle-
sticks, many odds and ends. TAKE AWAY EVERYTHING AT
ONCE FOR $700!

I scheduled it for a Sunday, thinking junk pickers from miles around would show up, but hardly anyone did. An old man swindled us out of the three-pronged cane by telling me it was for someone poor and crippled that he wanted to help.

"Oh, take it for free then," I said.

Then he walked away using it for himself. Why did he have to lie? I would have given it to him if he'd been honest.

An old Russian lady with an elegant apartment in your building bought the rug and a lamp. A few parties looked but bought nothing.

I ended up paying a junk company almost $300 to take most of it. Even the charity that supplied homeless vets with furniture only wanted the couch and the dresser.

They sent two guys to pick them up. I was in a victimy kind of mood.

"This isn't even my apartment," I complained. "I'm just trying to help a guy in a nursing home."

I felt put upon. I was getting nothing for my troubles except a bill from the junk company. But those guys, whose mission was "to bring the Love and Hope of Jesus Christ to those we serve," they gave me something.

"Yeah," one said with empathy in his voice. "It's a round world."

A round world. What comes around goes around.

God, I hope so.

THE BRIEFEST HONEYMOON

Your lover-boy period was short-lived. The anxiety returned. After many tries, your doctor came up with a cocktail of drugs that helped. But until she did, you drove everyone crazy.

It wasn't just the constant requests for blood pressure checks, though that was a big part of it. You required attention so often that your nurse tried to get you transferred to the super-crazy floor.

"He's too demanding," she said. "He needs more attention than we can give."

You'd started arguing with your doctor, which led to me being called to the principal's office to discuss your behavior. That was helpful because I realized that your doctor's sensitivity was as problematic as your attitude. She was taking your defiance as an attack on her skills.

"Stop making this about you, honey," I wanted to say. But I didn't. The new me.

Thank goodness for your nurse practitioner. Katie is pretty, blonde, short, and wears a white coat. You call her the Little Doctor.

She has no trouble handling you, then or now. When you asked her to check on you too often, she made appointments with you instead. When you acted out, she sympathized with you instead of scolding you. She knew you didn't need a transfer to the loony floor.

You were lonely, that's all. You'd bonded with a few other residents, but all of them soon moved to the fancy new facility. Your whole wing of the nursing home suddenly seemed primed for tumbleweeds. Rooms were empty. You sat by yourself in the hallway. Of course you got needy. Once again, you had to start over. How many times had you done it already, usually alone? In Auschwitz. In the DP camps. In America. When the deli closed. When your wife died. When Vera had her first stroke and couldn't speak. When she had her second stroke, then moved out. When you left home.

That's a lot of rebuilding on top of four years of torment. I don't think I could handle it.

I'd gotten a job, so I could only keep you company on weekends. I tried to find substitutes. I asked a local group whose aim is to keep Yiddish alive if they could find a volunteer to come chat with you in your native tongue. I never heard back from them. The Jewish service agency sent a volunteer visitor, but you refused to speak to him because he was a man. Who knew you hated men so much?

Then the Nazis gave you a present. I'd finally paid off both nursing home bills and all your old medical expenses, so your reparations were building up again. I started looking to hire someone to visit you, and when word got around to the aides and kitchen staff, a woman volunteered. I'd never met her before and didn't trust her one bit. What if she was out to swindle you? What if she mistreated you? But you trusted her. You were already friendly with Gloria. I think you two cooked up the plan to get her the job.

You'd always used your Nazi payout to be good to others. Now, by spending it on her salary, you were finally using it to be good to yourself.

SEPTEMBER 2010

"The people here are so old—*oy vey es mer!*" you'd commented as we walked the lanes of your new home and read the biographies of residents that hung outside their doors. The oldest one made it to 109.

Every year on her birthday, someone hung a diagonal banner over her door, announcing the achievement. This year, they displayed a poster on an easel in the main lobby. It had a photo of her in her wheelchair, the words HAPPY BIRTHDAY and the number 109, printed big and bold. Whoever had set up the public wishes had been quite excited about the lady's achievement, which was sweet, but I couldn't help thinking it was also a PR move: *See how good our care is!*

She didn't look 109, whatever that's supposed to look like. She had thick white hair, and though she sat very low in her wheelchair, she seemed only as aged as the women in their eighties. But she acted older.

For the more than three years that I observed her, I never heard her say anything but "Hello?" in a voice that was low and pleading.

"Helloww?" she growled. No one answered.

"Hel*loww!*" she growled again, angrier each time.

I didn't know what she wanted and the staff rarely responded to her, which really bugged me. The only other noise she made was a deep vibrato of a cough that sounded like the worst smoker you've ever met suffering from with the worst case of TB that's ever been diagnosed.

That lady freaked me out. I know I should have found it inspiring that she'd lived so long, but instead I found it disturbing. If I can't understand why you've been around for so long, what was I supposed to make of her? What was the purpose of her longevity? I hope she was a happy, beloved person for most of her life, but in her second century she seemed miserable. She looked to be suffering. I didn't want to see that. I didn't want that to be celebrated with posters and jolly birthday greetings.

One week I left your side and headed down the hall to put Gloria's check in your room. We'd agreed that I would leave it under the TV you never watch, transforming it into a TV-shaped paperweight. As I walked back, I noticed that the old lady's room was bare. The hospital bed was stripped, the shelves were empty, and the dresser was cockeyed, as if the movers had been in a big rush to get out. This didn't necessarily mean she had died. They were renovating the floor and people were continually being relocated. I peeked into the open doors as I walked back to you. A young woman with an old couple. A woman sitting on her bed, bent over her lap with her head in her hands. A frail form sleeping in a fetal position. But no old lady. Deaths are usually posted on a piece of printer paper taped to the wall, but I didn't see any notices.

I asked the nurse who was tapping pills into cups.

"Yes," she said flatly. "She died."

That's it? No sentimentality? No poster in the lobby announcing her passing? After 109 years, not even the printer-paper obit on the wall?

The absence of any mention of her death seemed incongruous with the hubbub that had surrounded her life. I couldn't figure it out. Was she that easily forgotten?

Hello?

Helloow?

The Fallen

The nurse called. You had fallen again.

No you hadn't. You'd placed yourself on the floor. Again. Because you're like a puppy that ransacks the trash when he hasn't been walked enough.

Here's how it played out. You waited until you thought no one was watching, then you slid your butt to the end of the chair and somehow lowered yourself onto the floor. No one knew exactly how you did this without plunking down hard and actually bruising your tailbone or cracking your pelvis, because no one had seen the lowering in action. The nurses had, however, seen you sitting quietly in the chair, then sitting quietly on the floor just seconds later. Never with an injury or an outcry. Just sitting.

You claimed you lost your balance, though how one does that in a chair is perplexing. It could have happened as you tried to stand, but I doubt it. Such a fall would have been far messier. Your walker would have rolled across the room. You would probably have been found on your back. And frightened. But none of that occurred.

The nurses are convinced that you do it on purpose. I hate to tell you, but I agree. Except for the time the aide saw you slip while putting on your pajamas, I think all of your falls have been sit-down strikes. But what are you protesting? Loneliness? Your body's stubborn hardiness? Lack of attention?

Or is it more extreme? I've heard that when everyone was being loaded onto cattle cars, some people deliberately sat down on the train tracks because they knew the guards would shoot them in the head and get it over with. Is that what you're up to when you hit the floor?

"I'm just disgusted with the whole life," you said on your last birthday.

Nah. I think you just want to create drama, which is exactly what happens every time you "fall." Whenever a patient goes down, the nurse is required to tell the family and write a report. But first she must get the patient up, which often requires a mechanical lift.

Then you're surrounded by action. Nurses and aides stop what they're doing, ignore other patients, and work on raising you off your rear. You get a talking-to, because the nurses are fed up with this scheme. But that must not be too bad, either, because regardless of their harsh words, at least they're engaging with you. You are a man again, in an argument, rather than a task wearing diapers.

Or maybe you're simply bored. My office mate heard my end of the conversation the last time a nurse called to report a fall.

"Were you talking to someone about a dog?" she asked after I hung up.

I told her the story, which didn't surprise her at all.

"Well," she said, "it's something to make the day pass. You can't just eat and poop."

2009

Dear Zelda,

Aron gets good physical care here. Mental? Not enough. I've been asking them to send him a counselor for two years. They say they're short-staffed, but I think they don't see the need. They see dementia and don't think anything can be done about it. Maybe they're right.

I've noticed that he's been fading lately. It's as if he's a hot-air balloon that's tethered to the Earth by a certain number of cables. Each cable is still quite strong, but there are fewer of them as time progresses, as if they're snapping one by one. When the last one frays and breaks, he will float away from me.

For the first time since I've known him, he looks like a Holocaust survivor—a recent one. I sat by his bed the other day while he napped and could almost imagine what those American soldiers saw when they met him: sunken eyes, cheekbones sharp and high. His face was all straight planes with no warmth or roundness. He even looked to be bald because his head was so deep in the pillow.

He's been obsessing about his pains again. He usually spares me, but the staff says he's constantly complaining of stomach or chest or leg pain. They give him as much of a sedative called Ativan as his body can take, but his anxiety laughs and carries on.

"How about some counseling?" I suggested again this morning.

He's going to die soon. And he's probably more scared than the typical elderly person because his fear of death has been festering for so long. With some counseling, maybe he could get the tiniest grip on it. Normalize it somehow.

"That's a really good idea, Sue," the medical authority of the day said. "I'm going to put in an order for that."

Really? Counseling hadn't crossed anyone else's mind? In the words of your son: Look what I got to put up with.

Love,

Sue

JANUARY 9, 2011

What's your take on heaven today? Sometimes, like religion, you think it's bullshit.

"When you're dead, you're like a piece of wood," you said not too long ago.

But I like your other explanation better, the one you gave me in various iterations throughout our friendship. The one that promised you'd have the power to return.

"I'll be with you in your dreams," you've reminded me.

I'm counting on that.

April 2009

You were asleep in your hallway chair when I arrived. When I tapped your shoulder and whispered your name, you opened your eyes. But you weren't fully with me yet. It was as if you fell deep into another world whenever you slept and the further you traveled, the longer it took you to return.

When you finally got back, you were miserable.

"I wish, like when I go to Birkenau—I wish to die," you said.

Every time you talked like that and behaved like that, I thought I'd lost the real you forever. But you kept surprising me. Like the time I ignored your complaints and talked instead about a problem we'd been having with a neighbor after Max and some friends exercised their throwing arms in the direction of his abandoned property. The boys apologized, got punished at home, and offered to pay for the damage to the rotting house's ancient windows, but the neighbor still called the police.

"You're upset," you said.

I was shocked. Not only had you heard what I was saying, but you had read what I was feeling. You knew why I'd told you the story: not to pass the time or to get advice, but because I needed a metaphorical pat on the back from a friend. Lo and behold, you patted. Then you even got witty about it.

"Between me wishing to die and Max with the windows, you got your hands full," you said with a chuckle.

NOVEMBER 2009

Sometimes you actually were sick. Once I found you perched in a wheelchair in front of your room instead of near the nurses' station. You looked quite happy, as if you were waiting to check people into a conference or distribute brochures of some kind. But it was lunchtime and you were wearing a bib.

"What are you doing down here?" I asked.

"I got a cold," you said.

But it was more than a cold. Gloria emerged from your room and told me you'd been swabbed for swine flu and were in quarantine until the results came back.

Why hadn't they told me?

Weren't you hysterical? For once, a real illness.

Yet you seemed perfectly fine. "Everyone gets sick," you said. "You get better or you don't."

That's when I knew the body snatchers had struck. Where was my Aron?

The worst part of your illness was that your voice was weaker than ever. You'd been speaking very quietly for a while, as if after nearly ninety years your vocal cords or diaphragm were too tired to push a message all the way out. Your lips moved, but the sound seemed stuck behind your teeth. I had to lean in and strain to hear you, especially on that day. The words I caught sounded like gibberish. Or Yiddish. But I could hear some English in the middle of phrases.

"Are you speaking in Yiddish?"

You smiled, partly embarrassed and partly entertained by yourself.

"It's a good language."

I don't think you'd realized that you'd fallen back into it, but once I pointed it out, you didn't seem upset. I, however, was completely rattled. If you were going back to the land of Yiddish, weren't you moving farther away from me? Was this a sign that the end was near, like when dying people speak to their mothers right before the end? And even if it wasn't the end, what if you lost your English before you died and we couldn't talk anymore?

JANUARY 9, 2011

It's so quiet in here. Where are all the *meshuggeners?* I used to scold you when you referred to the other residents that way, but in many cases, you were right. Whether due to age or genetics, many of them are *nutty.*

Let's review.

"Do you know how I can get the ferry to New York from here?" a man asked me last month.

"Nope," I said.

I'm so bad with directions. Plus, we were in the middle of a nursing home in Massachusetts.

At least he was in a good mood. That same guy, the one who pushes his wheelchair with his feet, a la Fred Flintstone, had it out for you last year.

"Be very careful of this man," he said to me as he pointed at you. "He's a very dangerous man."

"He thinks I killed his wife and daughter," you told me with annoyance.

Then he looked at me with his asymmetrically set eyes and asked me how Pearl was. Who the hell is Pearl?

The lady with Alzheimer's was much more pleasant. She may have lost her sense of time, but she hadn't lost her enthusiasm or inflections. Listening to her was like spending time with a wise relative who cared enough to give advice—somebody else's wise relative, because none of her statements applied to me.

"That's exactly what your mother used to say," she said to me one day. We hadn't been speaking prior to her comment.

"Yeah," I said. "I know."

She looked well: neat gray hair, matching outfits, occasional teeth.

"You should always listen to your mother," she added, a little more firmly. "You've only got one mother."

I didn't tell her that I'd lost my mother five years earlier because I didn't want her to stop. It amazed me that she could still be delightful despite spewing nonsense.

Your nonsense sometimes delighted me, too. Like the time you started rambling about "grease for Axel."

"Who's Axel?" I asked

"You so smug!" you barked. "You go to college and know nothing about axles. I'm talking about a cart with a horse."

Oh, really? That's what we were talking about? I guess I'd missed the entire beginning, middle, and end of the conversation.

Then you turned to your table mate.

"She's a professor."

"Of what?" he asked.

"Bananas."

Now that's entertainment.

The doctor explained that you have vascular dementia, which can come from small strokes and bring on sudden drops in brain function. But instead of a sudden or gradual decline, yours has been choppy, as if you're walking long stretches of flat land then suddenly trip and fall off a cliff.

Once she hypothesized that your cataract was disorienting you. That made sense; you couldn't see your world well, so you saw another.

You were having a conversation the first time I witnessed it. You looked toward the chair in your room and spoke to Bibi. It was hard for you to give her your full attention because you believed Vera was standing behind you, talking at the same time. And I kept asking questions, too.

"What is Bibi saying?" I said.

"You ask her."

"Umm, why don't you?"

You turned to face her, mumbled something, nodded your head, then returned to me.

"I can't hear her."

No matter, because it was time to go. You were anxious to get to Rosenberg's bakery, which you claimed was somewhere out in the hallway.

"It's down the street," you said, as if I was blind.

I guess it was hard for me to see because the real Rosenberg's bakery was actually down a street in Zychlin in 1940.

When we got to the hallway—or the sidewalk in front of the bakery, in your case—you had a lot to tell me. Such adventures were happening at night! You ate pancakes with a bunch of men. You had to dodge a guy who was out to get you because you'd accepted a blanket from his woman and he thought that meant you were fooling around with her. The guy was nuts, you said with a gleam in your eyes, and not just toward you. You said he wanted to shoot you and "the other Jewish fellas."

All of this should have broken my heart, but it didn't because you told it with the joy and animation of a child disclosing a secret. I hadn't seen you that happy in—ever. Despite worrying about the guy with the gun, you were content. You'd built a world that included your hometown, your late wife, and your absent girlfriend. Who was I to interfere?

FRUIT

I didn't realize how bad your hoarding had gotten until you started smuggling fruit to me.

"In the dresser," you whispered, peering around for the authorities. "Take the bag."

"What bag?"

"Shhhh!"

"What bag?"

"Just take it. Don't ask questions."

The bag contained two apples, three oranges, and a banana. Bruised, mushy, and squashed. Yum.

I appreciated the gesture, though I tossed the fruit out as I left the building. The next week, you unfolded a napkin to reveal a pear that you'd hidden in your walker basket.

"Take it."

"I don't need it."

"Take it! I got it for you."

I thanked you again, but said you didn't have to steal fruit for me. I didn't want you to get in trouble. It was bad enough that you were throwing their napkin inventory off.

Your basket is always stuffed with paper napkins. Also, sugar packets. Rolls of wild cherry Life Savers spill out of all your pants pockets. Multiple cups of water slosh around your tray.

Sometimes the head of nursing confiscates the collection, but you build it right back up again.

I understand the impulse, the need for a survivor to accumulate stuff, just in case. But why napkins? How the hell can paper napkins save anyone?

JANUARY 9, 2011

I feel like there are things I should be doing. Vera should know what's going on. Shall I run down to get her? That would mean leaving you, so no, not yet. It's incredible that she may outlive you. Then again, that lady is proof of women's strength.

You've been pretty stubborn about visiting her on the Russian floor. The last time you refused, I went alone. All the women down there look similar, like babies in a nursery, with their round faces, tiny noses, and spiky pixie cuts. I found Vera, wheeled her into the hall, and told her you weren't with me because you didn't feel well.

"Aron," she said.

It was the first word I'd heard her speak in four years.

Then she pointed to the ceiling and I knew she wanted to go see you. Despite all she's lost, she was determined to get close to her man.

I couldn't get her all the way to your table because there were too many wheelchairs in the way, so I stayed with her in the doorway of the dining room. But you saw her, smiled, and waved. I called you over, but you wouldn't move. You must have been afraid you'd lose your seat. I stomped my foot and pointed to the floor, giving you the international sign for *Get over here!* You still didn't move. Now I was getting embarrassed. You were acting like a third grader. I excused myself and went to your side.

"Go see her."

"No."

"She came all the way to see you."

"I can't."

"Yes you can. You're being mean."

"So, I'm mean."

"You're hurting her feelings!"

You started to stand and I tried to help by pulling on your bicep, but neither of us was strong enough.

"Tell her I'll see her when I have more time," you said.

"What else should I tell her?"

"Tell her bye."

Charming.

"How about you love her?"

I know I shouldn't have been scripting the scene for you, but I couldn't stand watching you treat her like a stranger.

"Yeah," you said.

I gave you a look of disgust and began to walk away, but you weren't done talking yet.

"Tell her she was the best woman ever."

YOUR BIG BREAK (WITH REALITY)

They called me after you hit an aide, threw applesauce at someone, and bent back the fingers of your favorite nurse. "We need you to come," they said for the first time. "No one can handle him."

I jumped in my car and sped up the same road I took to get here today. It was easier that night, because after dark there isn't much traffic. When I arrived, you were in your wheelchair clinging to the handicapped bar on the wall. It was bedtime, but no one could get near you, never mind coax you to bed. You kept threatening to hit people away.

I was a little scared you'd get violent with me, too, so I approached carefully. You let me get whisper-close.

"You got to go," you warned in a panic. "It's not safe."

You told me the nurses were trying to kill you and that they'd kill me, too, if I didn't get out of there.

"Do you know who I am?" I asked.

You looked at me as if I were crazy.

"Yeah, you're Zoo," you said.

You were not happy that I was wasting time with such foolishness. I had to leave, you warned again. It was kind of sweet, the way you were trying to protect me.

You said you wouldn't go to sleep because you thought they'd put poison under your bed that would gradually snuff you out during the night.

They, I presumed, were the nurses on duty who seemed to think your behavior was another ploy for attention.

I'd dealt with one of these nurses before. In 2009, you developed a cataract in the eye that hadn't been blinded by the Nazis, making you effectively sightless in both eyes. The staff knew you needed the cataract removed, and I'd been told the procedure had been scheduled, but it seemed to be taking forever to get it done. Maybe they didn't realize how not seeing was diminishing you. You'd been genuinely falling a lot back then, sinking back into anxiety and walking around with food caked on your pants, which you would never have allowed if you could have seen it. Maybe they didn't know about the other eye. I went to the nurses' station to ask when the surgery was scheduled. It wasn't. The stern, stocky nurse was on duty.

"Everyone has cataracts," she snapped at me. "It gets scheduled when the physician decides it's necessary. When it's ripe."

"He can't see out of the other eye, either," I said.

"It's not an emergency," she said before turning her back to me.

And I once saw her scold you harshly when you dared to leave a chair she'd confined you to so you wouldn't wander the halls. Put the right uniform on her and she could easily pass for a female Nazi guard. I could see how you'd woven her and her team into your daymare.

I kept telling you that we were both safe—that no one was going to hurt us. You eventually agreed to let go of the railing and go to your room if I sat with you until you fell asleep. I had to get something from my car first—probably my phone—and I told you I'd be right back. I jogged to the main doorway that I'd entered and exited through every time I'd visited for years. Freely entered and exited.

The door was barricaded.

I couldn't get out.

Holy shit, I thought. Maybe you were right; they *were* trying to kill us.

I laughed at the thought, but also rushed to find another exit. Later I figured out that Security must routinely lock down the lobby after nine, but I'd never been there that late to experience it.

When I returned you were calmer. You let the nurse whose fingers you'd bent help you into pajamas. You let yourself fall asleep while I watched. The next morning, you were fine: not poisoned, not deranged.

That probably reinforced the nurses' belief that you'd been faking it. But the psychiatrist knew you hadn't. He said you'd experienced a psychotic episode that was probably caused by a post-traumatic flashback.

You didn't remember any of it.

DYING: AGAIN?

I used to believe every death threat.

Last year, I was helping you get into bed for a nap. I held your water cup while you drank because your hands were shaking so badly.

When you finally laid your head down, you held out your hand to shake mine.

"I'll say good-bye now," you said. "I won't see your face again."

I didn't know what to say. Were you serious?

"You'll still see me," I said.

"I'll see you on the other side."

Then you looked me in the eye with pure earnestness before closing your lids.

A week later, you were laughing with Max and asking if he had a girlfriend yet.

Your mind may have been wobbly, but your body was tenacious.

"His vital signs are stronger than mine," the nurses would say.

Your heart and lungs were strong even as you started to outlive your teeth.

I've always been so proud of your teeth. Their durability seemed like proof of your strong constitution. Tough guys don't need dentures.

Then right before you turned ninety-one, I noticed that the corner of your mouth was bloody. Or was that chocolate? Nope, blood. Your teeth had started to splinter and turn into pointy stubs on the bottom, so the dentist pulled the four front incisors, leaving only a string of stitching for your tongue to fondle.

But nothing on the inside seems splintered.

After I read a study that said some people may have a gene for old age that protects them against cancer and heart disease and other fatal stuff, I suggested you might have that gene and live another twenty years. You weren't thrilled with the idea.

"People pray to get old, but it's no good," you said.

Your grandmother, the one who knew Hebrew, used to pray that she and her grandchildren would get old.

I couldn't decide how to play it. Was it selfish to pray for you to live just because I dreaded living in a world without you in it? Did that mean I wanted you to continue suffering? It was as if you were continuously slipping on ice, suspended in the panic that moment contains, but you were never allowed to hit the ground and be done with it. Shouldn't I want that to stop?

Come on, God, I'd think, make a decision.

Whenever you bounced back, laughing and joking and flirting, I thought she'd decided to give you peace on Earth instead of in it. You still thought she was going the other way.

"I am very sick," you said to me over the phone one Wednesday morning.

I was in Rhode Island at the sticky beach house we rented, but you didn't know that. The staff noticed that you got extra anxious and needy whenever I went away, so they asked me not to tell you if I was out of town. I hated lying to you about my whereabouts, but I didn't want to add to your anxiety, so I went along with the plan. As long as I still visited you regularly and was always available by phone, you wouldn't figure it out.

"What doesn't feel well?" I asked.

"Very sick. I can barely move the feet."

"But you *can* move them."

How many times had we replayed this conversation? You get to ninety, you have a little stiffness.

I told you I would visit at the end of the week.

"I wish you could come today," you said.

"The end of the week is better," I said, fighting against the hurricane of guilt blowing through the phone.

"I'm very sick," you repeated. "I'll see you on the other side."

I decided to risk it.

"Or Friday or Saturday," I said.

DECEMBER 2010—JUST ANOTHER AFTERNOON OF HANGING AROUND WITH JAMES JOYCE

You were already at the dinner table when I arrived. Same seat, same position, same stare at the paper placemat. It was 3:45 on a Sunday. Dinner isn't served until 4:30 p.m., but almost all the tables were occupied. A movie was playing on the big TV, and the aides were busy passing out bibs, which added an illusion of life to the room. Still, most of the people appeared pretty close to death.

I placed a big box from Macy's in front of you.

"Happy Hanukkah!"

"What is it?" you asked. "Cookies?"

I told you to open it; you told me to open it, so I did. I showed you the slippers, nonskid on the bottom and wide enough to fit your feet, which look like rising dough that's overdue for a punch-down.

"Thank you very much," you said, affectless.

I showed you the flannel PJs.

"What size?"

"Large."

You nodded.

Next order of business: the check. Now that there are two Nazi checks—one from the opening act (the ghetto) and one from the feature (the camps)—it gets confusing. You'd signed a check last week. Now another?

You asked me to read the amount—they're getting smaller, though I don't know if that means our economy is better or Germany's is worse—then, with a shaky hand, you signed the eight letters of your name. You hesitated after the L. Had you forgotten what comes next? Were you going to sign *Libfrajnd,* your original name, instead of the one Bibi chose? Because making an error like that would have fit with the theme of the day, which seemed to be Yesterland.

"Were you in my town?" you asked. "Zychlin?"

This question came after several minutes during which you spoke words that I either couldn't hear or understand. Just words that didn't add up to cogent thoughts. Streams of consciousness. You'd turned into James Joyce.

"No," I said, "I haven't been to your town."

"How's your mother?" you asked.

"She's dead," I said. "How's yours?"

"How's your mother-in-law?" you replied, as if you'd simply inquired about the wrong person.

"She's dead," I said. "How's yours?"

Someone listening to us might have found my responses rude, but I knew what I was doing. Sometimes you need a dose of snarkiness. It's like when the Fonz whacked the broken jukebox. A bit of snark usually whirs you back into operation. You met my eyes and grinned.

Hello again.

You were back, but our conversational path was still meandering. Somehow we got on the subject of tall women. You remembered that in Zychlin, men preferred short women. A tall woman, "no matter how much money she had," wouldn't attract a husband. Which led, in your mind, to the most lonely girls of all: those in the camps.

Shaved heads. Skinny. Then some Joycean mutterings about their clothing, their monthlies, the rare possibility of getting pregnant.

"They'd get hanged," you said.

And black memories poured forth. You said something about a French Jew getting hanged, about Gypsies being killed, about Jews turning other Jews in, about pregnant women getting killed with their babies.

"Maybe if they were good-looking they'd give them to the Germans?" you asked.

Were you remembering this or speculating?

The topic jumped to your tattoo.

"The number. So if the Jew ran away they could find him and capture him."

An aide filled an unbreakable cup with apple juice. Another poured OJ. Someone on the other side of the room gagged for at least thirty seconds.

You thought about the Gentile prisoner at the camp who gave the tattoos.

"I don't know what happened to him."

You showed me on your plaid shirt with your finger how the man punctured your skin with a row of dots. Dot, dot, dot, you poked over your sleeve. After, you said, "the arm was all swollen."

A lady in a satin dress sang on the TV. The image was black-and-white.

"Aren't there any Christmas shows on?" a nurse asked.

Your words kept spilling out. They were quarters. We were in Vegas. "The best was Sunday. We had pea soup."

And then something about your brother taking a bowl used for beating eggs, filling it with soup, and hiding it under his bed. Your eyes twinkled. What wacky times you had in the camps! Or was this back in Zychlin, before the war?

A nurse served you a paper cup full of pills. After you sucked them down with some water, I wiped congealed saliva from the corner of your mouth with a napkin. You had more of them stuffed in your shirt pocket, of course, like silk handkerchiefs, and tucked into the waistband of your pants, like pistols. Collect enough napkins and you turn into Al Capone.

An aide rolled a tall silver cart full of hot food past us. You nudged my arm.

"Okay now," you said, pointing your chin at the windows. "Go before it's dark."

I hugged you tighter than usual. What was all that purging about, that final testimony? I thought I'd heard all of your memories, but new details kept seeping out. Maybe you needed to be thoroughly wrung dry before you could surrender.

I left you to dinner, to bed, to new slippers.

"I'll see you next week," I said, hoping I was right.

And in my head, I prayed: *Don't go. Don't go. Don't go.*

DECEMBER 15, 2010—HAPPY BIRTHDAY, SWEET 91

Dear Adolf,

This morning Aron Lieb, né Libfrajnd, graduate of Auschwitz, who your staff left to die in Dachau in April of 1945, turned ninety-one years old.

You lose.

Regards,

Sue

215

I was pretty excited about your birthday even if you weren't. I'd reminded you of it on my previous visit.

"I'll see you Wednesday," I said, "for your birthday."

"Ah, birt'day," you said, perking up for the first time since I'd arrived. You'd been slouched and mumbling for about an hour. *Chest pain. The feet don't go. Half past three.* Then the nurse brought you water, applesauce, Tylenol, and a constipation-syrup cocktail. You could focus again.

"Ninety-one," I said. "It's a big one."

"Twenty-one," you said.

You looked across the table at your dining companion, a tall man with brilliant blue eyes, and pointed your chin at me.

"If this is my friend, you should see mine enemies!"

You weren't as cheery on the big day.

"All my friends from my town died, and my brother is sicker than me," you said.

I worry that you're about to die when you're sick and weak, but also when you're coherent and uncharacteristically affectionate, like when you touch the tip of my nose or call me darling. I think your relaxed state means you've stopped fighting, a sign that Death is in the waiting room. I guess what I'm saying is that I worry about you dying all the time.

But on your birthday, I started to believe that you might be the last one standing—that if you'd survived this long, maybe you'd be with me for a long time: until Maxeleh's wedding, until Carrie is standing in a lobby, cradling a baby. I told myself to stop worrying about when you were going to die.

That's always when they get you, isn't it? When your guard is finally down.

JANUARY 2, 2011—ONE WEEK AGO

Your eyes were scary holes, barely opened.

"Where's Bibi?"

"She died," I said, as gently as I could. "You lost her in 1992."

You were still confused.

"She's sleeping," I amended.

"Where's Vera?"

"Downstairs."

"I have no one left to love."

Later, when you came back to me, I tried to get you out of bed and down to the dining room. It was almost dinnertime, not too crazy early to claim your seat. You sat on the edge of the bed and tried to stand. You couldn't push yourself up with your big hands, and I couldn't pull you with my weak ones. Nothing worked.

"You put a dog to sleep in this condition," you said.

I hunted down your aide and brought her to your room. She scolded you, as if you were lazy.

"Aron, get up! You can stand."

Jeez, lady, ease up a little.

But her harsh tone worked. You stood.

She left and you said you needed to pee before heading down the hall. I helped you toddle into the bathroom and stood behind you to make sure you didn't fall. Your stream was still strong, but your aim, not so good. You left a puddle on the floor. Like a dog.

I grabbed towels from the cart outside your room and mopped the floor. We stood outside your door, ready to walk the hall you'd walked a thousand times before to the meal you never missed.

"Please," you pleaded. "Let me go back to the bed. Please."

"Of course," I said and led you back.

I should have known that this was the final crumbling of the mortar that was holding the final brick in place.

You asked me to cover you. The puffy green comforter I'd brought from your apartment was folded in a corner. I pulled it up to your chin, kissed your forehead, and told you I was going to visit Vera. You asked when she'd be up.

"Later," I said.

And the last time I saw your eyes fully opened, you looked at me like a little boy watches his mother, with a mixture of fear and trust, as she closes the bedroom door after the final lullaby.

NOVEMBER 28, 2010

Six weeks ago, we were sitting in the hallway talking about the usual nothing. You wanted batteries for your electric razor. You asked me to buy a necklace for Gloria for Christmas. Then we sat in silence for a while, as we often did, just being together.

"That's the whole story," you finally said, referring to nothing.

But it wasn't. A chunky young woman wearing tight corduroy pants walked past us and out of hearing range.

"The thing is," you said, as if winding up for a profound soliloquy, "women today have such big behinds."

This is how I want to remember you.

JANUARY 9, 2011

Your room is getting busier. Nurses' aides keep coming in to comfort Gloria and to stand at the end of your bed and gawk. They're reverent, almost shocked, that after all your preamble—all your *I-think-this-is-the-days* and *it-was-good-to-know-yous*—this really could be it. You open your eyes for a moment, encouraging Gloria.

"He is waking up!" she says, popping out of her seat. "Look . . ."

But you close them before she can finish.

One of the nurses gives you a shot of morphine. She tells me that it's not a big dose, just enough to make you comfortable, and that later they can increase the amount if you need it.

Your panting slows. Now there are long pauses between each breath. It's natural for bedside vigil sitters to hold their own breath during such pauses, thinking *He's gone* with each period of silence. I'm not falling for it. I've been at deathbeds before, and I know this game can go on for days. Besides, I see your pulse tapping like a nervous finger in your neck, so I know you're still with me.

I let go of your hand and look away to find Bill's number in your address book. I'm standing a foot away from you, listening to Bill complain about how sick he feels, too, when it happens.

The nurse walked in, stood at the foot of the bed, and looked at your face.

"He's gone," she said.

Nice touch, waiting until your blood family and your heart family are around you before exiting.

I kissed your head, the soft little hairs so like the fuzz your mother's lips must have felt at the beginning. Warm. I touched your hand. Cold. Your skin had already turned yellow. You were wax.

I'd said good-bye to Bill abruptly without telling him you had died, but I called him back a few minutes later.

"He always had life in him," he said. "Always laughing."

Then, his voice breaking, he added, "I'm the only one left."

In less than a month, you would be laughing together again.

The doctor came in and made it official. The nurse took the mask off your face, but the indentations the elastic straps had made remained. There was no blood flow to plump your skin back.

Gloria started to cry. A social worker appeared.

"Would you like him to have an autopsy?" she asked gently.

Why? I wanted to ask her. *So I can see what a shredded human heart looks like?*

The Dive

You squinted your eyes so only a disk of color, slate-blue like an infant's, showed. Your focus at that moment may have been as limited as a newborn's, too, or you may have seen everything: her, me, the people you'd loved in that apartment by the sugar factory. Then, after you'd recognized that this was your last living moment, you dove. And we marveled: at the grace, the speed, the soundless break of the water—all in such contrast to every practice session that came before. For you had rehearsed this move, stepped right to edge of the board, so many times, in your mind and in truth. You thought it would be loud, painful, clumsy. You were wrong. It was beautiful. Because of all that practice? Or because you finally, finally caught a break? Absolutely unknowable. Well done, my friend. Well done.

THAT MOVIE, AGAIN

The part of my favorite movie, *Same Time, Next Year,* that makes me cry the most is something that doesn't happen: The characters don't stop seeing each other. But because it ends when they're old, you know that one day the affair will stop because one of them dies. And I imagine how horrible that would feel—to have found that one person in the world who gets you, and to lose them.

Now I won't have to imagine.

We didn't have an affair, and we were never apart for long periods of time, but the rest fits. You were my special person. You understood me like nobody ever has, and you loved me still.

"You could always see through me," the man said.

"And I've always liked what I've seen," the woman replied.

I don't think anyone gets more than one of those per lifetime, do you?

JANUARY 9, 2011

"Take your time," the blue-eyed nurse said, leaving Gloria and me with your body.

So, of course, we started to clean.

The social worker said someone could pack up your stuff and store it so I could go through it later, but I wanted to get it over with. Plus, I worried that they'd lose something sentimental.

"You'll have a big job after I'm gone," you'd predicted. "It will take you a week."

Yet the bulk of the job took less than an hour. We probably sorted quickly so we didn't have to look too closely at your body in the bed. Not that we wanted you gone—not yet.

We started with the pictures on your shelves. They paint a portrait of your life in America and of your fashion savvy: you and The Little Doctor posing for a nursing-school recruitment brochure (green hat, navy sport coat); you and Vera dolled up (paisley tie and matching pocket square); you grinning behind bottles of Smirnoff and seltzer at a party to celebrate the anniversary of the European end of the war (tweed blazer, yellow sweater vest); you with Max in your lap, both smiling brilliantly (white short-sleeved business shirt); you with Bibi on her graduation day (leisure suit); your wedding portrait (double-breasted gray); you with Bibi's entire family, posed on and around a sofa (spotted bow tie).

I took the print of an apple orchard painting that I thought would remind you of your childhood off the wall, and threw away the sports-car calendar that I'd bought you two years earlier.

Gloria found three gold utensils wrapped in a handkerchief in your top drawer. We didn't know they'd been a gift from Vera. Did you keep them for sentimental reasons, or for protection?

We found pairs of glasses everywhere. We found bags of candy bars and rolls of Life Savers.

I went through your closet. You'd told me that everything was junk except for the leather jacket, which will now keep Gloria's husband warm. I dug through all your pockets. Oh look, a napkin. A packet of sugar. A napkin *and* a packet of sugar. I took three shirts: one of the quilted flannel ones for Max, the green L.L. Bean for David, and a short-sleeved with stripes for me. The rest we donated. Someday I'll do the same with the overcoats and Bermuda shorts in my attic.

I found the green hat. It was on the top of your closet the whole time. Dammit. Thinking you'd lost it had made you so upset. But maybe this fact will help: Fein-Kaller, the 116-year-old Swiss store that had made and sold the hat, also went out of business in 2011.

The nurse came back. She said we had to leave so she could get you out of the room before her shift ended. I guess it's bad form to leave a dead body for the next nurse. I hadn't realized that she'd been waiting for us. I thought we were waiting for her. I guess we should have been keeping a bedside postmortem vigil instead of tidying.

She brought another nurse, two aides, and a gurney with her. A male aide offered to help, too, but they threw him out. It reminded me of a song lyric, "this woman's work, this woman's work," which I started singing along with Kate Bush in my head. They closed the door to do whatever one does to a body—tie up your jaw, slide you into a body bag, use the lift to transfer you to the gurney. I stood right outside. You know, side-of-the-road duty and all.

A lady who worked somewhere in the building came up and gave me a hug.

"We all loved him," she said. "May he rest in peace."

I had no clue who she was, but I was grateful. No one had touched me all day.

The door opened and they rolled you out, a blue velvet cloth over the shape of you.

The guy from the funeral home took it from there. All I had to do, he said, was get him an obituary in an hour if I wanted it in the next day's paper. Of course I did. What if your old friends or relatives wanted to come? I sat outside the dining room and started to write. Even though I was distracted by a lady reporting her previous night's incontinence to a nurse, I didn't want to leave. But I had no Internet connection, and I needed to find one so I could send the obit. I drove to a Starbucks, sat in the back, and got attacked by a song.

Keep me in your heart for a while, a weak voice warbled.

Fucking Warren Zevon. Leave me alone.

JANUARY 10, 2011
Dear Zelda,
Let me tell you how much people loved your son. The Little Doctor called me today to report that everyone on staff was in a daze.

"He will be so missed," she said. "He was such a presence. Even with his issues and the challenges of caring for him, everyone was attached to him."

Someone told me they even sent a grief counselor to talk to the staff about losing him, something that apparently never happens. That's how much of an impact he made.

Aron and I used to talk about why he had lived for so long. I used to suggest that he couldn't die until he had accomplished one final thing. We couldn't imagine what that thing could be, but maybe it was this: He was finally loved enough. The Nazis had filled him with their hatred, and it took a lot of years and a lot of people to flush it out and fill him with its opposite. Only then could he be sent back to you.

My job is nearly done. The social workers say that once the funeral is over, all I need to do to get him off the books are mail some death certificates out and pick up his TV.

"Now just enjoy your memories," she said.

I wish it were more complicated. I want reasons to return to the nursing home. There was a guy who came to visit his mother on Aron's floor every single day until she died. Then, he just disappeared. And even though I'd only talked to him a few times and never knew his name, I missed him. Now I'm the disappeared. Will any of them miss me?

I didn't expect it to be so easy to untangle myself from your son. When I was the executrix for my mother's estate, it took more than a year to deal with the paperwork. With Aron, I'll only need to close a bank account, shut off a phone, and cry.

But not yet.

I guess this is the last time I'll write to you. It's your turn, again, to take care of our boy. Good luck. I hope they have crullers up there.

Much love,

Sue

FEBRUARY 2011

Who saved whom?

I gave you a good death, but you gave me a good life.

You gave me value. You got me through the suburban years, the years when I had nothing to do but dissolve while my kids crystallized.

You were part of my life for fourteen years and five months—almost the whole span of my parenting. I went from nearly new mother to nearly finished (full-time) mother with you. When we met I'd been at it for fewer than four years, and now I have fewer than four years of active duty left. You provided a distraction, an intense counterweight to the tedium of motherhood. You gave me drama and a battle to fight and perspective. When things got tough, I remembered that my complaints had nothing on your life. Or your mother's. You may have even boosted my reputation around the house. Helping you, my kids told me, made them proud. I was doing something that mattered.

You gave me situations where I could shine and crises that made me feel important. You allowed me to be admired by strangers; you dug the kindness and patience from under my prickly surface; and you never made me doubt whether I was a good-enough friend. You picked me to take the ride with you.

You may have kept my marriage strong. When David and I were too busy building careers and human beings to notice each other, when I craved emotional intimacy, you were there. I never had the need to seek out a stranger. David wasn't threatened by the time and energy I devoted to you, though he admitted he may have been if you'd actually been thirty years younger.

I told a friend about you after you died. We'd been having lunch monthly for a couple of years, but I'd never talked about you. I don't tell many people about you partly because I don't even know what to call you—*my friend, my Holocaust survivor, this guy I take care of*—and partly because it usually results in discomfort: mine if they call me a do-gooder, and theirs if the subject of the Holocaust scares them.

But I needed to talk, and this friend is a good listener. She called our story extraordinary.

"I like to think everyone would do the same thing if someone similar came into their life," I said.

"Maybe," she said. "But most people don't have that opportunity. That's the extraordinary part."

The question now, as I move into the world without you, is this: What will I do with that value you bestowed on me? Does it stay in that bed in that institution, locked in like a memory, like all the good dead? Or do I fly away with it, fly like you never could, free as a bird, gone with the wind?

MARCH 2011

I didn't cry for two months.

Instead, I did useless things to swerve around the grief. I started swimming regularly for the first time since I'd met you, which I suppose was an unconscious attempt to connect with you again. I daydreamed about your bookend—the first boy who'd made me feel special, a kid from Colorado who grew up to spend time as a prisoner and a mental patient, just like you. I guess your type goes for the staid suburban girls.

Then the film of shock peeled away and I could feel again. I didn't like that. I'd had no idea how much space you'd created. I imagined vacuums drawing you out like a body part—an appendix, a tooth, a fetus—until my insides were painfully clean and empty. Raw. Cored.

After that, tears.

JANUARY 11, 2011—THE FUNERAL

You were the first one in your family to have a proper funeral. I'm proud to tell you that I didn't fuck it up.

I was so nerved-up, as you'd put it, so worried that I'd get something wrong. You'd picked out the coffin and the grave, but it was up to me to stage-manage. I took half an Ativan in your honor.

The cemetery is hard to find. It's close to main roads and high-ways, but also up a street in the middle of nowhere. The perfect place for a murder.

Two funeral home guys in black overcoats were waiting for us by the hearse. My father and stepmother arrived. Vera's daughter Anne and her husband. A lady from the gift shop whom I didn't recognize, but who told me you two had planned to run off together if only you'd been a little younger. You used that line on everyone, huh?

Your roommate's son and daughter-in-law showed up. A lady from the Jewish agency who claimed she'd visited you with a volunteer "semi-regularly" joined us. The male volunteer you'd rejected came, too. He has an appreciative woman client now, but he still respected and remembered you.

Gloria got lost, but I wouldn't let them start without her. It was sunny out, though still too cold for any of the snow to melt. Some crows were cawing wildly. Did I ever tell you that I believe birds are dead people come back to check on us? I came up with that one after my mother died and birds started to appear everywhere. Now I notice them whenever someone dies. Maybe these feisty crows were your family, or your school friends from Zychlin. I don't think you were among them. The night before, while we were lying in bed, David said, "If you listen carefully, you can hear an owl." That owl—you?—hoo-hooed for most of my sleepless night.

Gloria finally showed up with her extremely handsome husband. She looked like a movie star in her big sunglasses, wide-brimmed black hat, and completely coordinated black-and-gold outfit. We made our way to the hole they'd dug for you. Anne, Gloria, and I sat in the chairs they'd set up at its perimeter, and the funeral home guy covered us with wool blankets as if we were going for a carriage ride. Honestly, it was almost that nice.

The rabbi read some Hebrew, which I have to admit I find com-forting—as long as I'm not expected to participate. She asked if any-one had stories to tell about you. Anne remembered dancing with you at a wedding. Your roommate's daughter-in-law told everyone that the night before you died she overheard you talking to one of the nurses. She was talking about all the things she'd given up so she could lose weight, all the things she couldn't enjoy anymore.

"What about sex?" you'd asked.

The rabbi liked that. She called it life-affirming. She pointed out that despite your losses, you had used your outgoing nature to build yourself an extended family. There weren't many of us at your funeral, but we'd all come out of desire, not obligation. Not one of us was a blood relative of yours.

We read the Mourner's Kaddish, the traditional prayer for the dead, which says nothing about death. Instead, it declares God's greatness and asks for peace. As in all things Jewish, a bouquet's worth of theories explain why it's recited at funerals.

Then we stood by the pile of dirt as the rabbi explained the custom behind using the back of the shovel to scoop it.

"It shows our reluctance to fill the hole," she said. "Imagine how long it would take to fill this hole if you did it all that way?"

I showed my reluctance by spastically missing the hole and scattering dirt on the artificial turf surrounding it.

After everyone tossed a shovelful onto your coffin, I brushed off your flat, metal grave marker, complete except for the date they would add later. I placed a rock on it. Another Jewish tradition, to show that someone has visited the grave and that the deceased hasn't been forgotten. The kids added stones, too, and Max took one from the dirt pile and put it in his pocket.

It was Max's idea to finish the ritual with lunch at your favorite IHOP. On the way, I asked him what he'd learned from all the years of knowing you.

"It's important to flirt and be nice to people," your little Maxeleh said.

It was a great funeral, Aron. You would have been so pleased. No side of the road, no piles of bones. Not even tears, at least from me. I was psyched: You got the death you deserved—quick, dignified, maybe painless—and I got to keep my promise.

There were only a couple of wrinkles to the day. The funeral directors and the grave diggers had trouble wheeling the gurney holding your coffin from the hearse up the snowy hill leading to the gravesite. It kept skidding and getting stuck in ruts. None of them could figure out what to do, as if it was their first funeral. Eventually, they decided to go old-school and carry the box by hand.

When they got you to the top, they prepared to lower you into the cement-lined hole. There were planks for the men to stand on as they centered you over the hole, but one of the pieces of wood must have been loose, because a young grave digger lost his balance. He let go of his corner of the coffin, forcing the other three to shift so you wouldn't get too jostled. He was suspended over the hole for a few moments while everyone stopped moving and breathing, all of us wondering what we'd do if he actually tumbled six feet under.

The other men had to put you down to make sure he was okay, then lift and center you properly. They must have been rattled, because they struggled with that, too.

Once I saw that the grave digger hadn't been hurt, I got pissed. Clumsiness was threatening the dignity of your burial. Their mishaps messed with your remains. Didn't they know what your body had been through? Must you be knocked around even in death?

Then I realized that you might have appreciated the spectacle. Maybe you'd enjoy knowing that you were too much for them to handle—that it wasn't so easy to get you into the ground. Hitler failed. These guys couldn't bury you.

And neither can I.

The End

Acknowledgments

David, Carrie, and Max: I love you more than any human beings on Earth.

Dad, Isabel, Andy, Linda, Sam, Meri, Rita, Erik, Sydney, and John: You're a very close second. Thank you for helping Aron, and for supporting me always.

Alice Martell, who manages to be a fantastic agent and a human being at the same time: I am so lucky to have found you. I'm never letting you go.

Lara Asher, who has edited two of my three books: I am so grateful that Aron brought us back together for this one. To have a smart, dedicated editor who I can talk to and who listens to me is every writer's dream.

Jeanette Eberhardy, Emilie Haertsch, and Debbie Hagan, my wonderful Goucher writing group: We may be young, but I predict a long, fruitful life. Thank you for all of the spot-on suggestions.

The Berman family: Thank you for taking Aron into your hearts and keeping him there. I couldn't have handled him without you on both of our sides.

And to all the other good guys: the congregation of Temple Sinai, Sharon, and other generous souls; Rabbi Joseph Meszler; Lance Ackerfeld and JewishGen; Robert Housman; the German Consulate in Boston; Dr. Suzanne Salaman; Dr. Eric Sawitz; Lauren Keefe, NP; Mrs. Cynthia Joseph; Mary Dutton Pluhar; Harold Klingsberg; Barry and Michelle; Paul, Debbie, Michael, Heidi, Andrew, Karen, Noreen, Gene, and everyone else who gave Aron stellar care during his nursing home days.

God: We'll talk.

About the Author

Susan Kushner Resnick teaches creative nonfiction at Brown University. Her most recent narrative nonfiction book, *Goodbye Wifes and Daughters* (University of Nebraska Press, cloth 2010, paper 2011), earned her the Best Woman Writer 2011 prize from the High Plains Book Awards. The book also won a gold medal for nonfiction from the Independent Publisher Book Awards, and was a finalist for the Montana Book Award and the Western Writers of America Contemporary Nonfiction Award. Her first book, *Sleepless Days: One Woman's Journey Through Postpartum Depression* (St. Martin's Press, cloth 2000, paper 2001), was the first PPD memoir written by an American author. She's been a journalist for twenty-seven years, reporting most recently for the *Providence Journal*. She's been published in the *New York Times* magazine, the *Boston Globe*, *Parents, Utne Reader,* and *Montana Quarterly,* among other publications. She was nominated for a Pushcart Prize in 2001, and her work was listed as a notable essay in *The Best American Essays 1999*. She lives in Massachusetts with her husband and two teenagers.

To see photos of Aron Lieb throughout his life, please go to www.susankushnerresnick.com.

ML   10-12